SADDLE, SWORD, & GUN

~~ THE LOCHLAINN SEABROOK COLLECTION ~~

Everything You Were Taught About the Civil War is Wrong, Ask a Southerner! - Correcting the Errors of Yankee "History"

Honest Jeff and Dishonest Abe: A Southern Children's Guide to the Civil War

A Rebel Born: A Defense of Nathan Bedford Forrest - Confederate General, American Legend (winner of the 2011 Jefferson Davis Historical Gold Medal)

Nathan Bedford Forrest: Southern Hero, American Patriot - Honoring a Confederate Icon and the Old South

The Quotable Nathan Bedford Forrest: Selections From the Writings and Speeches of the Confederacy's Most Brilliant Cavalryman

Give 'Em Hell Boys! The Complete Military Correspondence of Nathan Bedford Forrest

Forrest! 99 Reasons to Love Nathan Bedford Forrest

Saddle, Sword, and Gun: A Biography of Nathan Bedford Forrest For Teens

Abraham Lincoln: The Southern View - Demythologizing America's Sixteenth President

The Unquotable Abraham Lincoln: The President's Quotes They Don't Want You To Know!

Lincolnology: The Real Abraham Lincoln Revealed in His Own Words - A Study of Lincoln's Suppressed, Misinterpreted, and Forgotten Writings and Speeches

The Great Impersonator! 99 Reasons to Dislike Abraham Lincoln

The Quotable Jefferson Davis: Selections From the Writings and Speeches of the Confederacy's First President

The Quotable Alexander H. Stephens: Selections From the Writings and Speeches of the Confederacy's First Vice President

The Alexander H. Stephens Reader: Excerpts From the Works of a Confederate Founding Father

The Quotable Robert E. Lee: Selections From the Writings and Speeches of the South's Most Beloved Civil War General

The Old Rebel: Robert E. Lee As He Was Seen By His Contemporaries

The Articles of Confederation Explained: A Clause-by-Clause Study of America's First Constitution

The Constitution of the Confederate States of America Explained: A Clause-by-Clause Study of the South's Magna Carta

The Quotable Stonewall Jackson: Selections From the Writings and Speeches of the South's Most Famous General

The Quotable Edward A. Pollard: Selections From the Writings of the Confederacy's Greatest Defender

Encyclopedia of the Battle of Franklin - A Comprehensive Guide to the Conflict that Changed the Civil War

Carnton Plantation Ghost Stories: True Tales of the Unexplained from Tennessee's Most Haunted Civil War House!

The McGavocks of Carnton Plantation: A Southern History - Celebrating One of Dixie's Most Noble Confederate Families and Their Tennessee Home

Jesus and the Law of Attraction: The Bible-Based Guide to Creating Perfect Health, Wealth, and Happiness Following Christ's Simple Formula

Christmas Before Christianity: How the Birthday of the "Sun" Became the Birthday of the "Son"

The Caudills: An Etymological, Ethnological, and Genealogical Study - Exploring the Name and National Origins of a European-American Family

The Blakeneys: An Etymological, Ethnological, and Genealogical Study - Uncovering the Mysterious Origins of the Blakeney Family and Name

UFOs and Aliens: The Complete Guidebook

Britannia Rules: Goddess-Worship in Ancient Anglo-Celtic Society - An Academic Look at the United Kingdom's Matricentric Spiritual Past

The Book of Kelle: An Introduction to Goddess-Worship and the Great Celtic Mother-Goddess Kelle, Original Blessed Lady of Ireland

The Goddess Dictionary of Words and Phrases: Introducing a New Core Vocabulary for the Women's Spirituality Movement

Aphrodite's Trade: The Hidden History of Prostitution Unveiled

Thought Provoking Books For Smart People
SeaRavenPress.com

SADDLE, SWORD, & GUN

A Biography of Nathan Bedford Forrest For Teens

LOCHLAINN SEABROOK

WINNER OF THE JEFFERSON DAVIS HISTORICAL GOLD MEDAL

Sea Raven Press, Franklin, Tennessee, USA

SADDLE, SWORD, AND GUN

For ages thirteen to eighteen - Grades seven to twelve

Published by
Sea Raven Press, PO Box 1054, Franklin, Tennessee 37065-1054 USA
www.searavenpress.com • searavenpress@nii.net

Copyright © 2013 Lochlainn Seabrook
in accordance with U.S. and international copyright laws and regulations, as stated and protected under the Berne Union for the Protection of Literary and Artistic Property (Berne Convention), and the Universal Copyright Convention (the UCC). All rights reserved under the Pan-American and International Copyright Conventions.

First Sea Raven Press Civil War Sesquicentennial Edition: March 2013
ISBN: 978-0-9858632-6-5
Library of Congress Catalog Number: 2013934842

This work is the copyrighted intellectual property of Lochlainn Seabrook and has been registered with the Copyright Office at the Library of Congress in Washington, D.C., USA. No part of this work (including text, covers, drawings, photos, illustrations, maps, images, diagrams, etc.), in whole or in part, may be used, reproduced, stored in a retrieval system, or transmitted, in any form or by any means now known or hereafter invented, without written permission from the publisher. Te sale, duplication, hire, lending, copying, digitalization, or reproduction of this material, in any manner or form whatsoever, is also prohibited, and is a violation of federal, civil, and digital copyright law, which provides severe civil and criminal penalties for any violations.

Saddle, Sword, and Gun: A Biography of Nathan Bedford Forrest For Teens,
by Lochlainn Seabrook. Includes an index and bibliographical references.

Front and back cover design, interior book design and layout, by Lochlainn Seabrook
Typography: Sea Raven Press Book Design
Front cover image: "To the Lost Ford," © John Paul Strain
All other images © Lochlainn Seabrook
Portions of this book have been adapted from the author's other works

The views on the American "Civil War" documented in this book *are* those of the publisher.

The paper used in this book is acid-free and lignin-free. It has been certified by the Sustainable Forestry Initiative and the Forest Stewardship Council and meets all ANSI standards for archival quality paper.

PRINTED & MANUFACTURED IN OCCUPIED TENNESSEE, FORMER CONFEDERATE STATES OF AMERICA

CONTENTS

Notes to My Readers: 9
Introduction: 11

1 DEFENDING NATHAN BEDFORD FORREST: 13
2 FORREST'S CHILDHOOD: 16
3 TEENAGE FORREST: 21
4 FORREST GROWS UP: 24
5 HUSBAND & BUSINESSMAN: 28
6 SOUTHERN TYCOON: 31
7 FORREST & SLAVERY: 34
8 THE SOUTH SECEDES: 37
9 FORREST & LINCOLN'S WAR: 40
10 THE BATTLE OF FORT DONELSON: 45
11 CONFEDERATE DRAMA: 52
12 THE BATTLE OF FORT PILLOW: 57
13 "THE VERY GOD OF WAR": 63
14 THE TENNESSEE CAMPAIGN: 67
15 THE END OF LINCOLN'S WAR: 72
16 FORREST POSTBELLUM: 77
17 FORREST'S FINAL YEARS: 82
18 AN "UNTUTORED MILITARY GENIUS": 86
19 A BLUFF BEATS A STREIGHT: 90
20 "NATURE'S SOLDIER": 93
21 A HERO FOR THE AGES: 97
22 RIDIN' WITH FORREST: 103

The Forrest Home Fund: 105
Bibliography: 106
Index: 109
Meet the Author: 111
Meet the Cover Artist: 113

6 ∾ Saddle, Sword, and Gun

Dedication

To the millions who admire the Wizard of the Saddle. Because we know him, we love him.

"If your course has been marked by the graves of patriotic heroes who have fallen by your side, it has, at the same time, been more plainly marked by the blood of the invader. While you sympathize with the friends of the fallen, your sorrows should be appeased by the knowledge that they fell as brave men battling for all that makes life worth living for."

General N. B. Forrest, from an address to his troops in early 1865

NOTES TO MY READERS

☛ Keep your dictionary handy. Throughout this book I have purposefully used large and sometimes unfamiliar words in order that you, my young readers, will have an opportunity to enlarge your vocabulary and grow as students of history. Knowledge is power. Being informed is being smart!

☛ In any study of the "Civil War" it is vitally important to keep in mind that the two major political parties were then the opposite of what they are today.

The Democrats of the mid 19th Century were conservatives, akin to the Republican Party of today, while the Republicans of the mid 19th Century were liberals, akin to the Democratic Party of today.

Thus the Confederacy's Democratic president, Jefferson Davis, was a conservative (with libertarian leanings); the Union's Republican president, Abraham Lincoln, was a liberal (with socialistic leanings).

☛ The cause of the "Civil War" was simple: in essence, it was the South's limited government conservatism against the North's big government liberalism—or what Confederate Vice President Alexander H. Stephens called "Constitutionalism vs. Centralism."

This battle continues to this day. Only now it is a war of words rather than of weapons.

The pro-North movement will stop at nothing to suppress the facts about Lincoln's War and prevent you from learning what really happened between 1861 and 1865. As a result of their nefarious efforts, their version of events, the *Northern* version of Lincoln's War, has long been accepted as the final word.

However, the pro-South movement is coming to life once again after 150 years of near dormancy, and, as a Southern historian, I am proud to be doing my part to preserve authentic American history for future generations through my literary works.

For those of you who are interested in the Truth about the War for Southern Independence (that is, the *Southern* version of Lincoln's War on the Constitution and the American people), please visit the online store of my publisher, Sea Raven Press, where you will find a complete list of my titles, along with book descriptions and purchasing information.

SeaRavenPress.com

Nathan Bedford Forrest as a young man, the earliest known image of him. (Image © Lochlainn Seabrook)

INTRODUCTION

My cousin Nathan Bedford Forrest was, to me, one of the most interesting figures in American history, and certainly the most extraordinary officer in the War for Southern Independence, Confederate or Union. Many people from around the world agree. Even most of Forrest's Yankee enemies held a grudging respect for him, often bordering on awe.

Union General William T. Sherman, for example, declared Forrest "the most remarkable man our Civil War produced on either side." This is high praise coming from an individual who, during Lincoln's War, referred to the ingenious Rebel chieftain as "that Devil Forrest," and sent out an order to have him hunted down and killed like a wild dog! Sherman failed in his attempt of course, and went on to become one of Forrest's greatest supporters.

Despite the near universal admiration of General Forrest, no Confederate military man has been so insulted, so ridiculed, and just so plain misunderstood. As a Southern historian and author I feel it is my duty to educate these uninformed enemies of the South, which is why I have written six books on "Ol' Bedford" so far.

It is my hope that after reading *Saddle, Sword, and Gun*, my latest tribute to Forrest, you too will appreciate, even love, the one-of-a-kind, hell-bent-for-leather individualist who lived a short but amazing life, one that we today can only dream of. The rough and tumble Tennessean certainly made the planet a much more interesting place before he exited the world stage in 1877!

There will never be another Nathan Bedford Forrest. And that is as it should be.

Lochlainn Seabrook, Sons of Confederate Veterans
Franklin, Williamson County, Tennessee, USA
March 2013
Soli Deo Gloria
Luke 17:20-21

Confederate General Nathan Bedford Forrest, age forty-three, during Lincoln's War. Taken in March 1865, it is his best known photo. (Image © Lochlainn Seabrook)

DEFENDING NATHAN BEDFORD FORREST

THE GREAT YANKEE COVERUP

EVER SINCE THE END OF Lincoln's War and so-called "Reconstruction," the North—and her unenlightened friends here in Dixie—have been busily engaged in a truly nefarious process: whitewashing away the virtues of our Confederate heroes, while concealing the sins of the Union's. This is part of what I refer to as the "Great Yankee Coverup."

This conspiracy has been used to great advantage against both Rebel officials and everyday Southern citizens. In my opinion, however, no one has been more severely victimized by it than my cousin, famed Confederate cavalier Nathan Bedford Forrest.

POLITICAL CORRECTNESS
Though one would never know it from most of the books written about him, America has produced few individuals more remarkable, patriotic, and gallant than General Forrest. And yet, while he has legions of admirers, even worshipers, his detractors are many, and becoming more numerous with each passing generation.

This growth in the tide against Forrest can be attributed, in large part, to the modern phenomenon of political correctness, a movement that exaggerates, or more often invents, weaknesses and wrongdoings in high profile individuals in order to buttress its own social view and political agenda.

> Enemies of the South love to denigrate Forrest, no doubt because he is considered a hero here in Dixie, where he has always been loved and respected by enlightened people of all races.

It was inevitable then that one of the traditional South's favorite sons would become a target of the politically correct, who eagerly paint Forrest as an illiterate hayseed, undisciplined military officer, dour leader, violent sadist, underhanded businessman, crooked politician, unfaithful husband, and, above all, a racist cracker.

Their preconceived, prejudicial notions of him, their untenable, subjective evaluation of him by today's standards, and their utter lack of familiarity with life on the southwestern frontier of 19th-Century America, have turned Forrest into one of the most despised and misunderstood men in U.S. history.

FORREST THE EXEMPLAR
The demonization of the General as the "bad guy" of the Old South is both unjust and inaccurate, for despite his imperfections there is much about Forrest that is commendable. In fact one could say, with full justification, that Forrest possessed many traits that embody the loftiest qualities of humanity, making him an exceptional role model for the modern world.

Since Forrest can no longer defend himself, in this book I will speak for him. To do this, I will examine his traits and character in the context of his astonishing life story, one set against the backdrop of 19th-Century pioneer life and Abraham Lincoln's needless and illegal War.

General Nathan Bedford Forrest. Photo taken in December 1863. (Image © Lochlainn Seabrook)

FORREST'S CHILDHOOD

TENNESSEE BIRTH

FORREST WAS BORN, ALONG WITH a twin sister, in dire poverty in a dirt-floor log cabin on July 13, 1821, in the Duck River region near Chapel Hill, Bedford (now Marshall) County, Tennessee. This, his first home, was so primitive that daylight could be seen through the chinks between the logs.

> Forrest's twin sister, Fanny Forrest, was named after her aunt Fanny Beck (born about 1804), their mother Mariam's sister.

PARENTS

His father, William Forrest, was an English-American blacksmith from North Carolina; his mother, Mariam Beck, was a Scots-Irish-American pioneer whose parents were from South Carolina. Both descended from rugged, independent-minded, vigorous, hard-working European stock, traits they passed onto their firstborn son.

THE AGRARIAN LIFE

Like the majority of Southern families at the time, the Forrests were small-scale yeoman farmers who grew crops such as corn, wheat, oats, and cotton. They owned livestock as well, mainly horses—which the young Forrest was particularly adept at caring for and riding—along with cattle, mules, and chickens.

FORREST'S THREE NAMES

Forrest's personality can be understood, in part, from his three names.

> In ancient and Medieval times, the forester who guarded a private woods was often not paid. Instead, he was given special privileges, such as the right to keep his farm animals in the woods, or gather up and use any branches (for firewood) that had been knocked during inclement weather.

His first derives from his paternal grandfather, Nathan Forrest, a tough English-American pioneer from Orange County, North Carolina.

His middle name, Bedford, comes from the Tennessee county he was born in.

The surname Forrest is English and derives from the Old English *forest* ("woods"), and can be either a toponym for "one who lives in or near a forest," or a metonymic occupational name for "one who works in a forest" (i.e., the "keeper of the forest").

It would appear that his original family surname may have been Forrester, as some of his earlier ancestors spelled the name in this fashion.

Either way, the surname Forrester is also English, with the same etymology as Forrest, but with the specific meaning, "an officer in the charge of the forest" (Forrester can also sometimes mean "a worker in the forest").

From this we can be quite certain that one of Nathan Bedford Forrest's earliest English ancestors was either a forest worker or a watchman over a royal family's private forest, and that this individual probably spelled the name *Le Forester* or *DeForest*.

One of his probable paternal ancestors was Sir Thomas Forrest, an Englishman of royal blood, who settled at Jamestown, Virginia in 1607, while on the maternal side Forrest could claim Celtic blood through his Irish and Scottish forebears.

Names are destiny, and as such, for the rest of his life Forrest's would deeply connect him with family pride, manly honor, his Tennessee origins, his Southern roots, the great outdoors, and his royal Anglo-Celtic heritage.

CHILDHOOD & EDUCATION

Born into rural impoverishment with no time or funds for formal education, Forrest never experienced childhood as we know it today. Instead, he entered adulthood almost as soon as he could walk, child labor being a necessity among early pioneer families. Indeed, he was already a seasoned frontiersman before reaching his teens.

> Unfortunately, the house in which Forrest was born did not survive into the present day, having been torn down long before even the 20th Century, perhaps as early as the mid-1800s.

While his childhood peers were attending the local public school, Forrest was being "home-schooled" by life on America's Western frontier. Mother-Nature was his "teacher"; the wilderness was his "classroom"; and clearing land, farming, hunting, and buying and selling livestock were his "lessons."

Shopping at the local general store was out of the question for an indigent family like the Forrests. Instead, everything was either grown or made on their farm. Adolescent Forrest sat up at night making buckskin clothing, shoes, and hats for himself and his family members by candle and firelight.

FORREST'S BOYHOOD HOME

In his ninth year (1830), Forrest's father William moved the family onto a parcel of land owned by Mr. W. S. Mayfield of Chapel Hill, Tennessee.

On the property was a log and frame house ideally suited to their way of life. Along with the house came a variety of outbuildings, barns, corn cribs, a stone-lined well, several barbeque pits, a limestone fence, and a frame smokehouse. Limestone caves, open farmland, and deep woodlands provided entertainment and good hunting for the Forrest children.

Here young Forrest would receive the first three months of his six month education at the local schoolhouse.

The Mayfield residence, today known as the "Nathan Bedford Forrest

Boyhood Home," still stands. It is being restored and preserved by the Sons of Confederate Veterans, who plan on opening it up to the public.

"Our Confederate Heroes and Our Confederate Flags."
(Image © Lochlainn Seabrook)

Reunion of Forrest's Escort, Lynchburg, Tennessee, probably in the 1890s. There are at least three black Confederate soldiers in attendance. (Image © Lochlainn Seabrook)

TEENAGE FORREST

MISSISSIPPI, DEATH, & FAMILY RESPONSIBILITIES

THREE AND A HALF YEARS later (in 1834), thirteen year old Forrest and his family changed residences once again.

This time, with an eye toward advancing his station in life, William moved the household to Tippah County in northwestern Mississippi. The small parcel of land, which lay not far from what used to be the village of Salem, was located on the Tennessee border in a wilderness area that had recently been purchased from the Chickasaw.

> Land was not "stolen" from Indians, as Yankee history books tell us. White settlers bought it from them, often at exorbitant prices.

Three years on, in 1837, William died suddenly, and Forrest, though only fifteen, was the eldest son, making him the head of the family. Literally overnight the teenager became the father figure of a thirteen-person clan, one that included three sisters, six brothers, his aunt Fanny Beck, and his mother Mariam (who was five months pregnant with her eleventh and last child, Jeffrey).

Though this would have overwhelmed most young teens, Forrest was anything but a typical boy. In fact, the youngster took to his new role with surprising enthusiasm and maturity. Pledging to care for the whole group, he worked relentlessly as a menial laborer, supervising the farm and his mother's affairs—all while receiving his final three months of rudimentary schooling.

Due to his "robust constitution," "resolute soul," "unflinching industry," clear, good sense, and thrifty management," the Forrest homestead began turning a profit for the first time in years, giving the family a level of financial security and comfort previously unknown to them.

HARD WORK & ILLNESS

Despite this success, this period of Forrest's life was one of unending toil and hardship. Surviving his first fifteen years was a feat in and of itself: all three of his sisters (including his twin) and two of his eight brothers perished from disease (typhoid fever) while still in their youth. Forrest himself almost died from the same illness, but recovered, imbuing him, at an early age, with a strong sense of fortitude and good luck, and a true appreciation for life.

> Like most farm boys, Forrest attended school during the Winter months, between the harvest and planting seasons, when he was least needed at home. In his case, Forrest's entire period of education, three months in Middle Tennessee and three months in Mississippi, took place during the Winters of 1836 and 1837.

Tennessee backwoods. (Image © Lochlainn Seabrook)

General Forrest.
(Image © Lochlainn Seabrook)

4

FORREST GROWS UP

TEXAN SOJOURN

IN 1841, FORREST'S TWENTIETH YEAR, his mother Mariam remarried, to Joseph Luxton, and had four more children, three sons and a daughter, Forrest's half-siblings. In February of that same year, with the responsibility of heading the family now turned over to his stepfather Joseph, Forrest answered the call to help Texas win her independence from Mexico.

He had no way of knowing that the Mexican-American War would not begin for another five years. Yet, hearing of local skirmishes along the border, he excitedly enrolled as a volunteer under Captain Wallace Wilson at Holly Springs, Mississippi. The troop then headed for New Orleans, where, besieged with money and transportation problems, it disbanded.

> The Mexican-American War lasted from 1846 to 1848. It was won by the United States.

Undaunted, Forrest pressed on with what was now a small group of eager tenderfeet. By the time they arrived in Houston, however, the border clashes had dissipated, and soldiers were no longer needed.

Having spent his last penny, the disappointed young man worked on a Texas plantation splitting rails (for 50 cents per 100) for four months to earn enough money for his return trip home.

A LIFE CHANGING EPIPHANY

As he was traveling back northward up the Mississippi, he had a remarkable, life altering experience: standing on the steamer's deck, he was mesmerized by the many large, beautiful cotton plantations that dotted the riverbanks. There and then he decided that one day he too would become a wealthy planter.

Coming from someone like the indomitable Forrest, this was no idyllic daydream. It would become a reality—come hell or high water.

LEAVING HOME & FAMILY BUSINESS

By Autumn 1842 some of his family members were moving westward to DeSoto County, Mississippi, and so Forrest, now twenty-one, left home for good and settled in the same region to pursue his passion at the time: livestock trading.

> Like many young men today, Forrest was in a hurry to go out into the world and prove himself.

Fortune soon smiled on the young, uncultivated Tennessean, for his uncle, Jonathan Forrest, offered him a partnership in his livery and horse-trading business at Hernando.

Their flourishing partnership would be all too brief, however.

Just three years later, in March 1845, Jonathan got into a dispute with a man named T. J. Matlock, Esquire, his two brothers, Jefferson and James Matlock, and an overseer named Bean.

Not used to mincing words, and always one to defend his kin, the young hot-headed Forrest inevitably found his way into the middle of the argument, staunchly standing up for his uncle.

Voices and fists were raised, and soon pistols emerged. In the ensuing melee Jonathan was killed and, in response, the athletic and wiry Forrest unflinchingly killed two of the Matlocks with his double-barrel pistol, and wounded the third Matlock with a Bowie knife tossed to him by a quick thinking bystander (Bean wisely fled before Forrest could get hold of him). Indications of Forrest's future as a gifted and fearless military officer were already becoming evident.

SHERIFF FORREST

While his two surviving attackers were imprisoned without bail (and later tried and found guilty of murder), Forrest was arrested then immediately released since he had acted in self-defense.

His pluck and charisma did not go unnoticed by the grateful people of Mississippi. Overwhelmed with thanks and adulation by the townsfolk, the courageous youth—who had taken on and beaten four thugs by himself—was promptly elected constable of Hernando and coroner of DeSoto County.

> Forrest was widely known as a fierce defender of his family. Once, as a youngster, he hunted down and killed a panther that had attacked his mother Mariam and his aunt Fanny one day while they were riding their horses through the woods.

Forrest's boyhood home, Chapel Hill, Tennessee. (Image © Lochlainn Seabrook)

Forrest in 1850.
(Image © Lochlainn Seabrook)

HUSBAND & BUSINESSMAN

A MEETING OF DESTINY

ONE SPRING MORNING IN 1845, shortly after his uncle's death, fate blessed Forrest once again when he came upon a horse and buggy stuck fast in a mudhole along a swollen creek. The carriage contained two elegantly dressed women: Elizabeth Montgomery and her pretty eighteen year old daughter Mary Ann—a sophisticated high society girl who was related to both Sam Houston, legendary Texan, and Richard Montgomery, hero of the American Revolution.

> One of Forrest's strongest traits was perseverance, a quality that brought him much success, both on the domestic front and later on the military front.

After courteously receiving their permission, he carried them to the safety of terra firma, then waded back into the water. Putting his shoulder to one of the buggy's wheels, he encouraged the horses forward, muscling the vehicle free and back onto dry land. The two refined ladies, from nearby upper-crust Horn Lake, Mississippi, were grateful, but leery. Who was this pushy, coarse, but chivalrous backwoodsman?

COURTSHIP & MARRIAGE

An assertive opportunist, Forrest lost no time in pursuing the young Montgomery girl, still fresh from the famous Southern school, the Nashville Female Academy. A short courtship ensued, and on September 25, 1845, Mary Ann's uncle and legal guardian, the noted clergyman of the Cumberland Presbyterian Church, Reverend Samuel Montgomery Cowan, married the young couple in Hernando. The local newspaper announced that Forrest's wedding had been accompanied by "a good sweet morsel of cake and a bottle of the best wine."

CHILDREN

The next few years would be the happiest of Forrest's short but amazing life. Settling in with his new bride, the family quickly grew with the birth of their first child, William Montgomery "Willie" Forrest, in 1846. The following year, 1847, brought more hope for a bright future with the arrival of their second and last child, Francis Ann "Fanny" Forrest.

> Forrest was twenty-four years old and Mary Ann was nineteen years old at the time of their marriage in 1845.

MEMPHIS

In 1851 Forrest closed the mercantile business he had shared with his Uncle Jonathan and resettled his little family in the thriving river port of Memphis, Tennessee, a move that would have profound repercussions, both positive and negative, for the rest of his life.

ENTREPRENEUR FORREST

Despite his lack of proper schooling—he had had only six months of public education—Forrest evinced an amazing proclivity for making both money and friends. Throughout the 1850s he started numerous businesses in rapid succession, including a stage line, a brickyard, a construction company, and a livery and stable operation. He also dabbled in railroads, insurance, real estate, and farming supplies, and by 1852 he had entered into the occupation that would transform his life: slave trading.

A DAUGHTER'S DEATH

The year 1854 brought personal tragedy into Forrest's world. On June 26 his six year old daughter Fanny died of "flux" (dysentery). This could have been nothing short of devastating for the thirty-three year old father, who was known for his deep love of family and children.

Forrest and his men cutting down another meddling Yankee outfit. (Image © Lochlainn Seabrook)

SOUTHERN TYCOON

POLITICS

A FEW YEARS LATER, NOT CONTENT to be merely a supportive and reliable husband, a doting father, and a successful businessman, Forrest got into politics: in 1858 Memphis eagerly elected the lanky rough-and-tumble Tennessean to the office of alderman, where he energetically pushed through new legislation, even setting up the town's first commercially viable fire department.

REAL ESTATE

In the meantime, Forrest was fast becoming a real estate mogul of unprecedented proportions, buying up every available piece of acreage he could afford. On one occasion, for instance, he purchased 1,900 acres of prime cotton-growing land for $47,500—today's equivalent of $1,400,000. He patiently waited a few months, then sold it for three times what he originally paid—a winning strategy that he repeated many times.

> Forrest did not know it, but he was a descendant of European kings and queens.

It was during this period that he bought several plantations in Mississippi. The first was a small farm in Tunica County. The second, called "Green Grove," was an enormous 3,000 acre farm possessing a tidy six-room house and twelve cabins (that housed thirty-six of Forrest's servants), located in Coahoma County.

MILLIONAIRE

Forrest's hard work, native intelligence, endearing social graces, and vast business connections soon paid off. By the time he was thirty-seven years old, in 1858, the grayish-blue-eyed entrepreneur was earning a staggering $96,000 a year from slave trading alone, the equivalent of about $2,700,000 today. In 1859, for example, he sold approximately 1,000 slaves at $1,100 each (today worth $30,000 each), an earning of $1,100,000, or by today's standards, $30,000,000.

> Like many modern Southerners and Britons, Forrest typically dropped the "g" from the end of words; hence, he said "walkin'" instead of "walking." He also used the word "betwixt" instead of "between," "fetch" instead of "bring," "fit" instead of "fought," and "mout" instead of "might." Forrest also tended to spell phonetically. For instance, he wrote "hir" for "her," and "hed" for "head."

His cotton sales were bringing in untold millions more. "Green Grove" by itself was producing some 1,000 bales of cotton a year, earning Forrest $30,000 annually, today's equivalent of $900,000. By 1860 the Mississippi plantation had become so productive that some 200 field servants were needed to run it.

According to Forrest's own statements, he was worth $1,500,000 at the start of the War, or what today would be about $40,000,000. Considering that he owned thousands of acres of real estate, numerous homes and plantations, and hundreds of servants, and dabbled in dozens of other businesses, this figure is no doubt conservative.

Thanks to Forrest's ingenuity, industry, and enormous slave force, he had become not only one of the most successful slave traders in Tennessee, but one of the wealthiest tycoons and largest plantation owners in the U.S.

Confederate Major David C. Kelley (left) and Forrest (right).
(Image © Lochlainn Seabrook)

FORREST & SLAVERY

FORREST & HIS BLACK SERVANTS

IN FORREST'S BELOVED DIXIE, WHERE less than 5 percent of the population owned slaves, and where slave trading was considered an honest (if not the most desirable) way to make a living, he approached the North's "peculiar institution" (American slavery got its start in New England in the early 1600s) simply as an occupation. This is not to say that he treated his human property like chattel. Quite the opposite.

> Under the Constitution, slavery was legal across the entire United States in the 1850s, both North and South. So why do some people criticize Forrest for owning slaves?

Firsthand accounts from slavers who purchased from Forrest reveal that his servants were clean, well groomed, and well dressed, and that he encouraged them to learn to read and write (quite unlike typical slave treatment in Yankeedom). His servants respected his authority and, in return, he treated them with humanity and dignity, even going out of his way to make sure he did not divide families.

Indeed, it was his routine practice to purchase all members of a slave household if need be, in order to keep husbands, wives, and children together. In many instances he was instrumental in reuniting slave families who had been separated. He also refused to sell to inhumane slavers, and kept a list of who to avoid.

The result was that not only did Forrest's servants never revolt or try to escape, instead they showed great pride in belonging to him. Indeed, market slaves who learned of Forrest's benevolent reputation actually begged to be purchased by him.

FORREST FREES HIS SLAVES BEFORE THE WAR
In 1859 Forrest shut down his real estate and slave businesses in Memphis, sold most of his slaves, emancipated many others, then turned his attention solely to his plantations. This was five years before Lincoln issued his fake and illegal Emancipation Proclamation (January 1, 1863) and seven years before the Thirteenth Amendment finally ended slavery all across the United States (December 6, 1865).

The anti-South movement, of course, never mentions Forrest's personal antebellum emancipation proclamation, nor the fact that the philanthropic businessman got out of the slave trading business in great part because of his slaves themselves. While the racist avaricious North only abolished its slave trade when it could no longer tolerate the presence of blacks and when it became unprofitable in the region, egalitarian Forrest abolished his at the height of its profitability in the South in early 1859. Why? Because his servants had come to him "in a body" with the idea of closing his slave trading business and opening up a plantation, where they could continue to work for him without fear of being sold to someone else.

> Calling Forrest a racist because he owned slaves is quite absurd, for tens of thousands of Northerners owned slaves as well, including Yankee hero Ulysses S. Grant. Yet Grant is never called a racist.

Thus, though they were technically free, nearly all of his emancipated servants chose to stay on with "Marse Bedford," as they continued to fondly call him.

General Forrest's staff. From top center moving clockwise: John P. Strange, William M. Forrest (the General's son), Charles S. Severson, James B. Cowan, John W. Morton, Gilbert V. Rambaut, Charles W. Anderson. Center: Matthew C. Calloway. (Image © Lochlainn Seabrook)

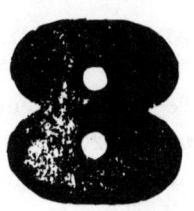

THE SOUTH SECEDES

LINCOLN & SECESSION

ON NOVEMBER 6, 1860, THE U.S. would change forever, and in the worst way possible: big government Liberal Abraham Lincoln became America's sixteenth president.

It was shortly after this date that South Carolina delegates called for a special secession convention. It was now clear that with a socialistic, anti-Constitution, anti-South progressive in the White House, the Southern states would, as they put it, "no longer have the power of self-government, or self-protection, and the Federal Government will have become their enemy."

On December 20, 1860, South Carolina left the Union, with other Southern states quickly following: Mississippi seceded on January 9, 1861; Florida on January 10; Alabama on January 11; Georgia on January 19; Louisiana on January 26; Texas on February 1. The Confederate States of America (C.S.A.) was officially formed on February 4, 1861, at the Confederate States Convention in Montgomery, Alabama, where a provisional government was set up.

After Lincoln took office on March 4, 1861, and began threatening to make war on the South, four more Southern states joined the C.S.A.: Virginia seceded on April 17; Arkansas on May 6; Tennessee on May 7; and North Carolina on May 20.

Two states wavered, with certain regions of each only joining much later: parts of Missouri seceded on November 2, 1861, while parts of Kentucky seceded on November 20. This made thirteen Confederate states, revealingly, the same number of American states that originally seceded from Britain in 1775. The coming conflict, incorrectly known in the North as the American "Civil War," was to be America's Second Revolutionary War, her second War of Secession, in fact.

> Abraham Lincoln was an anti-South Liberal who many in his own party considered not only insane, but completely unsuitable to be president of the U.S. It is little wonder that the conservative Southern states wanted to leave the Union upon his election.

As the Spring of 1861 approached, the president of the C.S.A., Jefferson Davis, and his Congress drew up their Constitution and prepared to move forward as a newly formed "Confederate Republic"—the same name George Washington gave the U.S.A. in the 1700s.

Lincoln was not happy. By separating from the Union and seizing important, strategically placed Federal properties, he was about to lose the South's enormous revenue stream (i.e., taxes). Just as importantly, secession was angering his financial backers, the North's famous "Wall Street Boys," the wealthy Yankee slave traders who had counted on conducting permanent business with the South's plantation owners. The South's departure also promised to interfere with Lincoln's plan to replace the Founding Father's conservative government with Henry Clay's liberal American System. One way or another, Lincoln maintained, the Southern states would have to be brought back into the Union.

Forrest's early home in Hernando, Mississippi. (Image © Lochlainn Seabrook)

FORREST & LINCOLN'S WAR

FORT SUMTER

AFTER "HONEST ABE" TRICKED THE South into firing the first shot at Fort Sumter on April 12, the world was left with the perception that the South had viciously "fired on the U.S. flag." Wanting war, this is exactly the reaction that Lincoln had hoped for.

> Lincoln committed numerous crimes in just the first few weeks of his war, including declaring war without congressional approval and illegally issuing a naval blockade in the South. He went on to perpetrate hundreds of other crimes over the next four years.

Northerners whipped themselves into a fever pitch of anti-South hatred. Millions of Yankees who, before April 12, had been for peaceful secession or who had been sitting on the fence, now fell squarely in behind their president, demanding retribution.

LINCOLN DECLARES WAR

Lincoln, who had preplanned the entire scheme with his war-mongering cronies in Washington, wasted no time granting them their wish. On April 15, 1861, he illegally issued a proclamation calling for 75,000 U.S. troops to invade the Confederacy and crush the "rebellion." King Abraham's war for the South's "subjugation, degradation and extermination" was on.

This overt act of aggression crossed the line, both literally and figuratively. As mentioned, on May 7, Forrest's home state,

Tennessee—which had been tentatively siding with the Union—angrily seceded. His adopted state, Mississippi, had already seceded much earlier, on January 9. Forrest could remain neutral no longer.

Liberal Lincoln would not give peace a chance, and so the South's conservative sons had no choice but to fight. Many of Forrest's neighbors felt just as he did, as he would later say in an 1868 interview: "I went into war because my vote had been unable to preserve the peace."

FORREST JOINS UP
It was at this flash point in American history, on June 14, 1861, that Forrest, along with his youngest brother Jeffrey and his son William, determinedly strode into the local recruiting office in Memphis and enlisted in the Confederate army.

Though prior to the War Forrest had been a "strong Union man" who was against Southern secession, Lincoln's unlawful attack was too much. A dyed-in-the-wool Southerner, a states' rights advocate, a free-trader, and a Constitutional conservative, Forrest was not going to stand by while Lincoln perverted the Constitution and transformed the government of the Founding Fathers from a "Confederacy" (the name of the U.S.A. from 1781-1789) into an empire—one of the Yankee president's primary goals.

The main problem, however, was financial in nature. Lincoln, who could not resist issuing anti-South policies, had been pushing for extra high tariffs to be applied across Dixie, an act that would surely have bankrupted many Southern businesses. Forrest, always the businessman, saw the South's economy in jeopardy and knew he had to act. Thus for Southerners like Forrest, supporting the new Confederacy was not just about Southern pride, true American patriotism, and "preserving the Constitution." It was also a matter of survival.

He wasted no time establishing himself with an army unit that Summer, at first serving as a private in Captain Josiah S. White's Tennessee Mounted Rifles Company. Seeing the appalling lack of supplies, like many other wealthy Confederates, Forrest outfitted and equipped soldiers wherever and whenever he could—once donating the modern equivalent of nearly $515,000 from his "personal funds" for pistols, saddles, and other much needed provisions.

> Forrest was born to be a soldier and quickly rose up the ranks of the Confederate military.

PROMOTION
Forrest's naturally keen grasp of military tactics and strategy, along with his elevated socioeconomic status (there were not many multimillionaire privates in the Confederate Army!) and sterling recommendations from the citizens of Memphis, impressed both Governor Isham G. Harris, Tennessee's only Confederate governor, and Bishop-General Leonidas Polk. Soon, despite his lack of military training, Forrest won a promotion to lieutenant colonel. His star continued to rise quickly and by October he was commanding his own regiment, "Forrest's Tennessee Cavalry Battalion."

FORREST THE RECRUITER
He also excelled at raising conscripts. Hundreds of Tennesseans, young and old, eagerly joined the Confederate army under Forrest's rousing promise that he would provide them ample opportunity to fight the "unscrupulous and vindictive foe." One of his recruiting posters read: "Come on boys, if you want a heap o' fun and to kill some Yanks!"

FORREST & HIS BLACK SOLDIERS
Contrary to Northern myth, Forrest was no respecter of race, which is why he enlisted his own slaves as well, seeing them as potential recruits in the South's fight against Northern liberalism and aggression. Knowing that the institution of slavery was already on its way out, he promised them their freedom at war's end.

Throughout Lincoln's illegitimate and needless four year struggle to overthrow the Constitution, unofficially as many as 1,000,000 African-Americans served (in one capacity or another) with the Confederacy—right alongside their European-American brethren. Dixie was, after all, their homeland as well, and the only one they had ever known.

Among them were sixty-five slaves serving in Forrest's command, forty-five of them belonging to the dashing officer himself. Of these forty-five brave men, he selected seven of the most elite to serve as his personal armed guard, a position they held until the end of the War. Revealingly, none of Forrest's black soldiers ever tried to flee or join the enemy, though they could have easily done so. To a man, all remained loyal to both Forrest and the Southern Cause through and beyond the conflict.

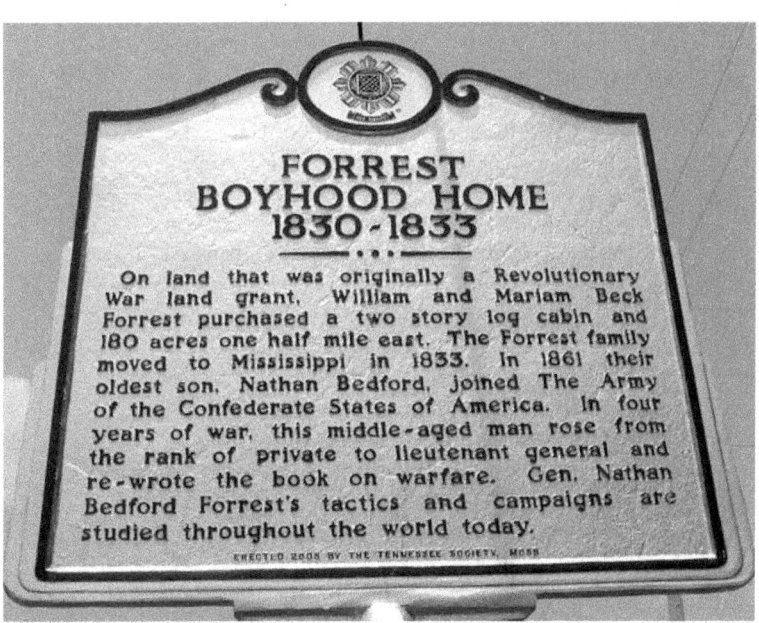

Historical marker outside Forrest's boyhood home, Chapel Hill, Tennessee.
(Image © Lochlainn Seabrook)

> **BY TELEGRAPH.**
>
> **DAY DISPATCHES.**
>
> **Gen. Forrest Tenders His Services.**
>
> MEMPHIS, December 9.—Gen. N. B. Forrest, in view of possible war with Spain, made a formal tender of his services to Gen. Sherman, who, writing a characteristic letter to Gen. Forrest, said he had sent the letter to the War Department with this endorsement:
>
> "Respectfully referred to the Secretary of War for file. Among the hundreds of offers that come to me, I deem this worthy of a place among the archives to wait coming events. I regard N. B. Forrest as one of the most extraordinary men developed by our civil war, and were it left to me, in the event of war requiring cavalry, I would unhesitatingly accept his services and give him a prominent place. I believe now he would fight against our national enemies as vehemently as he did against us, and that is saying enough."
>
> [Signed] "W. T. SHERMAN."
>
> General Sherman don't believe there will be war. Neither government wants war.

As this old newspaper clipping shows, in late 1873 Forrest offered his services to his wartime nemesis Yankee war criminal General William T. Sherman. At the time a possible war with Spain was threatening. Sherman turned him down, but kept Forrest's letter on file saying: "I regard N. B. Forrest as one of the most extraordinary men developed by our civil war, and were it left to me, in the event of war, I would unhesitatingly accept his services and give him a prominent place. I believe he would fight against our national enemies as vehemently as he did against us, and that is saying enough." (Image © Lochlainn Seabrook)

THE BATTLE OF FORT DONELSON

THE ENGAGEMENT THAT CHANGED THE WAR

THOUGH FORREST'S FIRST BRUSH WITH the Yanks was at Sacramento, Kentucky (December 28, 1861), his first major clash was against Union General Ulysses S. Grant at the Battle of Fort Donelson, Tennessee, February 11-16, 1862.

The consequences of the Confederate loss at Fort Donelson would haunt the South not only throughout the War, but into the present day, for this was no ordinary battle. It could even be said that Fort Donelson doomed the Confederate struggle from the beginning, which is why Forrest biographer John Allan Wyeth refers to it as "a blow which staggered the Confederacy and from which it is safe to say it never fully recovered."

Despite a skirmish that damaged Yankee gunboats and forced a Federal retreat, things looked grim for the Rebels, as Grant's reinforcements were now large enough to nearly encircle the fort. Forrest's superiors, Generals John B. Floyd, Gideon J. Pillow, and Simon B. Buckner, assumed there was no way out, and ordered a surrender of the fort. Never one to be easily intimidated, however, Forrest felt sure the garrison could be held—especially after he attacked and secured a Yankee artillery battery.

At a hurried and frantic war council held between 11:00 PM and midnight on Saturday, February 15, Forrest argued that since the Rebels were not yet surrounded, they were not yet beaten. In such a situation, he could not and would not give up the fight. Pillow, a soldier cut from much the same cloth as Forrest, now sided with his tenacious subordinate. Floyd and Buckner, however, held their ground, insisting on surrender.

The meeting was brief. Enraged at what he perceived as incompetence, Forrest roared "I did not come here to surrender my command!" He then stormed out, no doubt mumbling a litany of expletives.

Unwisely ignoring Forrest's ingenious plan to "whip the Yanks" by simply "marching out" under cover of darkness, Buckner remained at the fort with some 12,000 soldiers. Meanwhile, disregarding the order to surrender, Pillow abandoned Forrest and stole away across the Cumberland River on a small boat that night, while Floyd left early the next morning, with two Virginia regiments, on a steamer bound for Nashville. About 1,500 men escaped with these two commanders.

> If Forrest's superiors at the Battle of Fort Donelson had followed his plan, the Confederates would have won and Yankee General Ulysses S. Grant would not have become a Northern hero.

Forrest could not stand by and watch as the garrison was surrendered. It was not in his nature. And so, following up on his own plan, at about 2:00 AM, on February 16, he rode out of the fort, with some 1,500 Rebels in tow, and crossed the icy ford at Lick Creek toward the safety of Nashville. Forrest and his men saw no Federal troops during their movement out of Dover that night.

As the sun rose the next morning, Buckner found himself completely surrounded with no chance of escape. He had little choice but to capitulate to Grant's demand for "unconditional surrender," and in the ensuing Yankee "victory" Grant seized the fort, capturing 12,000 Confederate soldiers.

FORREST'S TACTICS EXPLAINED
To this day Forrest's critics call him a "coward" for this act. But far from being a yellowbelly, in truth he was one of the War's most brash and

fearless daredevils! Seeing the confusion and rancor among his commanders at Fort Donelson, Forrest saw no purpose in surrendering and facing imprisonment (or worse), and felt that this was a time when retreat was the better part of valor. Thus, his movement across the Cumberland avoided the needless wounding, capture, and deaths of hundreds of soldiers—many of them boys whose mothers he had promised to protect. Later, Forrest was wisely not punished for his insubordination.

CONFEDERATE ERRORS
Despite Forrest's foresight and bravery, the Confederate surrender at Fort Donelson will go down in history as perhaps the greatest and most crippling Rebel blunder during the first half of Lincoln's War.

To begin with, the surrender was indeed unnecessary. Scouts sent out to the area of Lick Creek ford on Saturday night, February 15, saw no Yanks in the vicinity. When Forrest himself crossed Lick Creek a few hours later, again no Federal soldiers were observed. As hundreds of Rebel troops moved out during the next few hours, according to the official record, none witnessed a single Union soldier anywhere in the region; none met with any opposition; none, in fact, came up against a barrier of any kind that would have prevented their escape. One Reb reported that there were no bluecoats even in the nearby town of Dover at the time.

Here then is conclusive proof that, since the Confederate surrender was made "under a delusion," it was completely unnecessary. Some 12,000 Rebel soldiers could have been spared capture and gone on to fight, probably successfully, at the Battle of Shiloh where, consequently, they were outnumbered by the Feds by nearly 20,000 men.

Second, the capture of Fort Donelson by the Yanks caused Rebel General Albert S. Johnston to relinquish Kentucky and most of Middle and Western Tennessee, all which had been controlled by the Confederacy up until that time. While this had a number of deleterious consequences for the South, one of its main effects was to allow further strengthening of Union control at Nashville (a primary U.S. nerve center). As we will see, this is something that would come back to mortally wound the C.S. at the close of 1864.

GRANT'S DEIFICATION AFTER FORT DONELSON

There was another even more significant reason that the needless Confederate surrender at Fort Donelson had such a negative impact on the South's chances for success.

As the Battle of Fort Donelson was unfolding, Grant's head was on the chopping block back in Washington. Both his Commander-in-Chief Major General Henry W. Halleck, and the General-in-Chief of the U.S. Army General George B. McClellan, were within a whisker's breadth of arresting and imprisoning Grant for

> Yankee General Grant was about to be arrested and imprisoned by Union officials in Washington, D.C. when he accidently won the Battle of Fort Donelson. This changed the entire War there after.

insubordination (disobeying orders), withdrawing from his command without leave, and traveling to Nashville without authorization. Of this situation Grant himself later admitted that

> "less than two weeks after the victory at Donelson the leading generals in the army were in correspondence as to what disposal should be made of me, and in less than three weeks I was virtually in arrest and without a command."

What saved Grant from certain court martial and imprisonment?

It was the unnecessary Confederate surrender at Fort Donelson, which handed the Union a complimentary victory. With this one stroke of fortune, Grant, though he had not earned it, became an instant hero in the eyes of the Northern populace, which both guaranteed him an eternal place in the military hall of fame and lifted the official accusations against him.

Even worse for Dixie, it allowed him to go on commanding throughout the rest of the conflict, during which time he cut the Confederacy in half at Vicksburg and committed countless war crimes (in conjunction with fellow war criminals Lincoln and Sherman).

Yes, Grant's brutal actions would inevitably secure him the dubious nickname "the Butcher," as well as the everlasting animus of the Southern people. But it was immaterial. For all of this would one day transform him into a Northern symbol of the 1865 Union victory over the South, predictably leading to his election to U.S. president in 1868.

As chief executive of the nation's second most corrupt administration (after Lincoln's), Grant then continued to wound and humiliate the South, supporting and maintaining the hellish Reconstruction period (1865-1877) with brute military force. (In gratitude, in 1913 Yankees placed his likeness on their fifty dollar bill.)

The fact is, however, that while Halleck and McClellan had legitimate grievances with Grant's defiant behavior, his most serious transgression was his extreme negligence in allowing Lick Creek and the surrounding area to be left unguarded throughout the night of Saturday, February 15, and the early morning hours of Sunday, February 16.

Considering the feelings of his superiors at the time, Grant would have almost certainly been arrested, demoted, and imprisoned had not Floyd and Buckner surrendered their army that same day, an act that transformed Grant into an international Yankee celebrity literally overnight—even earning him the unwarranted *nom de guerre*: "Unconditional Surrender Grant."

With his star rising and with renewed confidence, now backed by both the U.S. government and its people, Grant was able to go on to deliver one ruinous blow after another against the Confederacy, ultimately helping to seal her fate. He even lived to deliver the final humiliation to the South by being the one to accept Robert E. Lee's surrender at Appomattox three years later. All of this because Forrest's wisdom was ignored by his superiors on February 15, 1862. Wyeth put the matter like this:

> "Ten thousand men, armed and ready for battle, should have

marched out that night, and, with the boats which arrived in the early morning, three thousand more could have escaped across the river. Grant would have arrived to find the bird had flown. The empty fort and the artillery only would have been his. How changed would have been the pages of history if the plea of Nathan Bedford Forrest had been heeded by Generals Floyd and Buckner!"

In his official battle report Forrest stated:

"I am clearly of the opinion that two-thirds of our army could have marched out without loss, and that, had we continued the fight the next day, we should have whipped them. The roads through which we came were open [no Federal soldiers] as late as eight o'clock Sunday morning [the 16th], as many of my men who came out afterwards report."

Forrest was promoted to colonel on March 10, 1862, but it was of little consolation to him.

Another cousin of the author and another admirer of General Forrest: Confederate Vice President Alexander Hamilton Stephens. (Image © Lochlainn Seabrook)

Forrest ordering an attack. (Image © Lochlainn Seabrook)

CONFEDERATE DRAMA

THE BATTLE OF SHILOH

A**FTER QUELLING A FEBRUARY RIOT** in Nashville following the fall of Fort Donelson, Forrest went on to fight at the Battle of Shiloh, Tennessee, April 6-7, 1862. Here, he met up with Grant once again, a disastrous meeting for the Confederates that should have never taken place.

While Forrest's brilliant and violent rearguard maneuvers at Shiloh eventually forced the Yanks to retreat to Pittsburg Landing, the Rebs suffered nearly 11,000 casualties and the noble General Albert S. Johnston was killed.

Though the Confederacy was handed another defeat, Forrest used the Battle of Shiloh to introduce a bold new form of defensive fighting.

Galloping his horse out across the middle of the battlefield, he was shot in the side by a Federal soldier. The wound was excruciatingly painful (the bullet entered through his pelvis, nearly severing his spine), but Forrest ignored the injury. Instead, he reached down and grabbed the astonished rifleman by the coat, pulled him up onto the back of his horse, and held him behind him as a human shield.

The horrified bluecoats dared not fire at the brazen Confederate officer for fear of hitting their own man. Forrest escaped the field without further bloodshed, dropping his terrified attacker unharmed to the ground as he raced away. The legend of Nathan Bedford Forrest was just beginning.

BRAXTON BRAGG

On his forty-first birthday, July 13, 1862, Forrest achieved a particularly stunning victory at the Battle of Murfreesboro, Tennessee, where he routed and captured an army twice the size of his own. Referring to it as "my forty-first birthday present," the win garnered him another promotion: on July 21 he rose to the rank of brigadier general.

Despite these achievements, Forrest's commanding officer, General Braxton Bragg, largely ignored the ingenious cavalryman, offering not even a single word of praise. Thus began a long and rancorous animosity between the two, and they remained bitter enemies until the close of the War. Their heated arguments included yelling matches, up-raised fists, and even death threats. Things got so serious that Forrest was reassigned to another state. Knowing that the venturesome and combative Tennessean was invaluable to the South, Bragg, to his credit, never reported Forrest's insubordination to his superiors.

> During Lincoln's War, Forrest introduced new methods of fighting, inspired thousands of Confederate soldiers with his reckless bravery, argued with his superiors, and killed dozens of Yankees with his bare hands.

He did, however, "pay Forrest back" later when, while working under President Davis at Richmond, he devoted an inordinate amount of time to undermining Forrest's military career from behind closed doors. Tragically, this helped stall and even prevent Forrest's promotion to full general, while robbing the Confederacy of the comprehensive use of one of its most valuable, knowledgeable, and successful officers.

THE GOULD AFFAIR

While Forrest was fighting at Jackson (December 19, 1862), Parkers Crossroads (December 31), Thompson's Station (March 5, 1863), Brentwood (March 25), Franklin I (April 10), Day's Gap (April 30), and Black Creek (May 2), he continued to raise eyebrows and hackles, even among his own subordinates. One of these was Confederate Lieutenant

Andrew W. Gould, who was nursing an old grievance toward his commander over an imagined wrong.

On June 13, 1863, the young officer angrily cornered Forrest in a hallway at his headquarters at the Masonic Building in Columbia, Tennessee, stuck a pistol in his ribs, and pulled the trigger. Fortunately, the bullet only wounded Forrest, who then turned the tables on Gould, instinctively stabbing him in the chest with a small knife that he pried open with his teeth and one hand (he used his other hand to hold down his struggling attacker).

Suddenly realizing what he had done, Forrest tried to have the young man's life saved, but the wound proved too serious and Gould passed away a few days later with the General at his bedside. An individual at the scene later wrote:

> "Forrest wept like a child. It was the saddest of all the sad incidents of the long and bitter war I witnessed."

The great Confederate leader, after having the lead ball removed from his left hip without anaesthesia, quickly recovered. He had acted in self-defense and no charges were filed.

Still, heartbroken over the incident, Forrest made a pledge to himself that he would never kill another human being—except for Yankees, and then only in defense of the Confederacy.

CHICKAMAUGA, PROMOTION, & EMANCIPATION

At the Battle of Chickamauga, Georgia, September 18-20, 1863, Forrest scored numerous crushing blows against the Yanks and helped win the day for the South. However, to everyone's surprise, the military perfectionist felt that the Confederate victory had been won more by accident than by good soldiering, and he turned in his resignation. Sensibly, his superiors would have none of it and instead promoted him to major general in December.

This period marked another milestone in Forrest's life: though he had promised his forty-five slave-soldiers their liberty at the end of the War, witnessing their bravery, mastery of weaponry, and undeviating devotion to the South, he decided to emancipate them shortly after Chickamauga. All

> Forrest freed his slaves years before Lincoln's fake and illegal Emancipation Proclamation was issued.

forty-five proudly stayed on with their stalwart leader, happily spreading mayhem and killing Yanks alongside Forrest until the last day of the War.

Private Louis Napoleon Nelson was one of the dozens of African-American Confederate soldiers who proudly served under General Forrest during Lincoln's War. Louis' grandson, Nelson W. Winbush, wrote the foreword for my bestselling book: *Everything You Were Taught About the Civil War is Wrong, Ask a Southerner!* (Image © Lochlainn Seabrook)

Confederate Brigadier General Jeffrey Forrest, Forrest's beloved youngest brother, died at the Battle of Okolona on February 22, 1864, fighting for the Constitution and Southern honor. (Image © Lochlainn Seabrook)

THE BATTLE OF FORT PILLOW

A FABRICATED CONTROVERSY

AT THE BATTLE OF FORT Pillow, Tennessee, April 12, 1864, Forrest achieved one of his most stunning triumphs. Sadly, in the ongoing effort to malign Forrest's good name, Yankee mythographers later invented the story that a racist slaughter had taken place. To this day biased pro-North historians still insist on calling it not the Fort Pillow Battle, but the "Fort Pillow Massacre."

According to anti-South propaganda, Northern blacks (and whites) were allegedly tortured and crucified, or were gunned down during the act of surrender. Other reports claim that Confederates had buried wounded Union soldiers alive, and that theft of the injured and dead took place the night of the battle.

Since Forrest's critics maintain that his worst traits (allegedly "racism," "impetuousness," and "cruelty") were exhibited here, a cursory review of this conflict is in order.

THE ROLE OF ALCOHOL

There is little question that the South won a decisive victory at Fort Pillow. The question is how? Was it by brutality and deceit, as the North claims, or simply good soldiering, as the South maintains?

To begin with, many of the Yankee soldiers, in particular the black ones, were thoroughly intoxicated on April 12. Standing defiantly on the parapets, they taunted, jeered, shouted profanities, and made obscene gestures at Forrest's men, daring them to attack. In their thoroughly inebriated state they apparently felt immortal and refused to obey Forrest's usual command to "surrender or die." Unaware that the Federals were drunk, and observing their staunch resistance, Forrest's soldiers rightfully unfurled a "galling sheet of fire" upon them, and dozens fell.

> Enemies of the South love to accuse Forrest of war crimes at the Battle of Fort Pillow. But as all the official records show, he was totally innocent of any wrongdoing.

This incident only explains some of the Union injuries and deaths, however. There was another factor behind the hundreds of Yankee casualties, one that can be better understood by examining the enthusiasm with which Forrest's men attacked.

PERSONAL RETRIBUTION

Prior to the Battle of Fort Pillow, the U.S. soldiers who manned that garrison (a number who, like many of Forrest's men, were also from Tennessee) were known to have captured, tortured, and murdered men specifically from Forrest's cavalry. At least seven of the General's soldiers died in this manner, all suffering horrid deaths that are too gruesome to recount here.

Torturing and killing captured prisoners of war is, of course, illegal and immoral, as is torturing and killing non-combatants and civilians. But military and religious law did not prevent Billy Yank from engaging in both of these heinous practices.

Is it possible that on April 12, 1864, Forrest's men marched toward the "nest of outlaws" at Fort Pillow with vengeance on their minds? While such behavior cannot be condoned, if they did, it is certainly understandable. For Forrest's men the Battle of Fort Pillow was, after all, more a local feud than it was an impersonal fight with strangers. They knew many of the enemy personally, and before the War had been neighbors, even friends. The dismemberment, mutilation, and slaying of their fellow comrades in arms, along with the growing criminal activities of Northern troops in the area, no doubt weighed heavily upon their minds that Spring day as they approached the fort.

UNPLANNED INCIDENTS
There were other factors that contributed to the Yankee disaster at the Tennessee garrison, such as a confusing and difficult topography, as well as a series of unexpected events over which Forrest had no control.

For example, midway through the hostilities a segment of Yankee soldiers agreed to surrender, sending up white flags of truce. Only yards away, however, other Federal troops continued to pour canister into the Confederate lines.

About this time a number of boats, including a Yankee steamer and a Yankee gunboat (both packed with U.S. soldiers and artillery), chugged toward Fort Pillow's river landing, ignoring the white truce flags that were fluttering in the breeze in plain sight (under the rules of engagement, the boats should have come around and moved away).

Perhaps emboldened by the sight of their steamers plying toward the fort, those Yanks who had previously considered surrendering now decided to fight on, this time with renewed vigor. Oddly, and unfortunately for history, they left their Union flags of truce flying.

Mass confusion ensued on both sides, Confederate and Federal, and more unnecessary Union injuries and deaths occurred.

THE "BURIED ALIVE" MYTH
As to the charge that Rebels buried wounded and dying Yankees alive, it is patently false, as Federal forces were entirely responsible for burying their own. Far from participating in such atrocities, Forrest and his men helped carry wounded Yanks from the field, carefully and respectfully placing them in tents and barracks where they could be cared for by Confederate surgeons. The General himself was personally responsible for saving the life of at least one seriously injured Union soldier.

THE "ROBBERY" MYTH
Then there is the accusation that Forrest and his men raided and robbed

the fort after dark, stealing valuables from the dead and committing other outrages. According to official reports, however, Forrest and his cavalry were well clear of the area by 6:00 PM, and had made camp some two miles away. The General never again returned to the fort after that.

This particular rumor can no doubt be attributed to gangs of often despicable "bummers," foragers who roamed the countryside heartlessly preying on the casualties of war.

YANKEE DISTORTIONS

Later, Yankee newspapers distorted, exaggerated, and even concocted various events pertaining to Fort Pillow in an attempt to justify Northern hatred of the South. Though manifestly fictitious, since the racist "massacre" tale was particularly distasteful to freedmen, Lincoln and his government naturally made the most of the trumped-up stories (inciting more discord, racism, and violence), all of which have been handed down to us today as "fact" by pro-North historians.

THE TRUTH

It is obvious that Forrest himself could not have been part of the alleged "massacre" because, in the midst of battle, when one of his horses was shot out from under him, it fell on his leg, moderately disabling him for several

> Lincoln, Grant, and Sherman all promised to retaliate on the South if Forrest was found guilty of criminal behavior at Fort Pillow. But they never did. Why? Because Forrest was found innocent by a Yankee governmental committee that investigated the affair. Still modern critics continue to condemn him for outrages at the battle that never occurred.

days. Thus for most of the conflict he was some 400 yards behind the main lines. On at least one occasion when he did manage to reach the front, he ordered his troops to pull back and cease fire.

Right up until their deaths many years later, Forrest and all of his men indignantly denied any wrongdoing on April 12. This is understandable, for there was no "massacre" at Fort Pillow to begin with. For instance, Forrest's worst crime was supposed to have been gunning down surrendering Yanks. Yet, the Union soldiers at the fort never surrendered!

Additionally, 60 percent of the Union soldiers stationed there survived, hardly what could be called a merciless slaughter. The 40 percent who perished falls well within the norm for a garrison taken by assault. As for the high percentage of black Union soldiers who were killed, this is explained by the fact that most were drunk, and therefore unable to shoot accurately or take proper cover.

Obviously blameless, at the close of the War both Federal eyewitnesses and even the U.S. government cleared Forrest of all charges concerning Fort Pillow. Despite this, indictments of maltreatment and prejudice have been affixed to Forrest for fifteen decades for his alleged role in a nonexistent "massacre."

The truth is that Forrest ordered a cease fire during the battle, then arrested one of his soldiers who ignored the command. According to one report, Forrest even shot one of his own men for refusing to give quarter to the enemy. Later, he was instrumental in saving the Union wounded. Clearly, he had gone to extraordinary lengths to prevent any unnecessary bloodshed under complex and trying circumstances. Is this the behavior of a merciless killer?

As to the inevitable charge of "racism" that is always hurled at Forrest by the uninformed, let the facts speak for themselves: Forrest integrated his black soldiers directly into his command, while the Union officers across the battlefield from him at Fort Pillow segregated theirs (in obedience to Lincoln's bigoted military rules). And it was Forrest who bragged that eight of his most exceptional cavalrymen were black. Is this the behavior of a mindless racist?

Confederate General John Bell Hood misused Forrest on several occasions, accelerating the Confederacy's doom in April 1865. (Image © Lochlainn Seabrook)

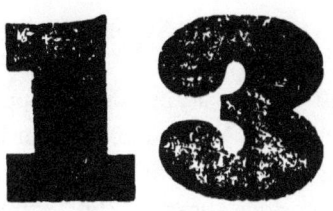

"THE VERY GOD OF WAR"

SHERMAN PUTS A DEATH WARRANT OUT ON FORREST

BY MID 1864 FORREST HAD several thousand soldiers under his command, a battle-hardened group known as "Forrest's Cavalry." The mere mention of his name now sent chills of fear and awe down the spines of Union officers.

One of these was General William T. Sherman, who confessed, with overt jealousy, that Forrest's clever maneuvers "excite my admiration." Sherman could not afford to stand by admiring Forrest for too long, however. A primary threat to Federal stability in the area, he put out the order for Forrest to be "hunted down and killed, even if it costs 10,000 lives and bankrupts the Federal treasury!"

To this end, Sherman sent U.S. Brigadier General Samuel D. Sturgis into northern Alabama and Mississippi with the sole purpose of getting rid of "that Devil Forrest," as Sherman called him. Sturgis was even offered a promotion if he killed the famous Confederate. But "Crazy Billy," like most of Forrest's own commanders, completely underestimated the charismatic, six foot two inch warrior. In what has become known as "the perfect battle" during the War for Southern Independence, Sturgis in particular would pay dearly for his arrogance toward "Ol' Bedford."

THE BATTLE OF BRICE'S CROSS ROADS
That "perfect battle," the Battle of Brice's Cross Roads, took place near Baldwyn, Mississippi, on June 10, 1864. Here, with a mere 3,200 men,

the audacious Forrest went up against, and whipped, Sturgis and 8,500 Union troops, forcing the Yanks into a disorderly and humiliating retreat. As always, in order to bring down the enemy, the astute tactician used his notorious "brag 'n bluff" strategy—a survival skill picked up during his childhood on the Western frontier.

With innate aplomb and stunning brilliance, Forrest commandeered his forces through one spectacular victory after another at Brice's Cross Roads, finally forcing the weary Federals into a desperate run for their lives. A master of the offensive who never received an attack but always launched it, Forrest greatly exaggerated the size of his command and strength of his fire power, chasing a terrified Sturgis through six counties on a rout that lasted some thirty hours.

> Forrest's presence on the battlefield always inspired his soldiers and petrified the Yanks!

At one point, between skirmishes, Forrest's nearly exhausted men were resting, hoping to hear the welcome order to "retire from the field." Instead their imposing commander approached them on horseback, looking fiery, energetic, and ready to do battle at a moment's notice. One of Forrest's soldiers, John Milton Hubbard, later recalled the scene:

> "Mounted on his big sorrel horse, sabre in hand, sleeves rolled up, his coat lying on the pommel of his saddle, looking the very God of War, the General rode down our line as far as we could see him. I remember his words, which I heard more than once: 'Get up men! I have ordered Bell to charge on the left. When you hear his guns, and the bugle sounds, every man must charge, and we will give 'em hell!'"

When the "hell" was over, Forrest had suffered only 492 casualties while Sturgis had suffered nearly 2,500. In addition, Forrest captured 1,600 prisoners (including sixty Yankee officers), sixteen guns, twenty-seven limbers, two colors, 184 animals, 192 wagons, 1,500 stands of arms, and a huge assortment of artillery and ammunition. Sturgis lost a third of his soldiers and all his trains—along with his dignity and any promise of promotion.

FORREST THE DESTROYER

Forrest went on to fight a host of other battles during the latter half of 1864, including Harrisburg (July 14-15), Memphis (August 21), Athens (September 23-24), and Sulphur Branch Trestle (September 25), awing soldiers on both sides with his majestic godlike presence whenever he appeared on the field of action.

Forrest was by now well adept, and well-known, for wreaking particular devastation on Union supply lines throughout the Western Theater. In his home state, for example, he broke apart railroad tracks, dynamited bridges, cut telegraph wires, fired warehouses, sank supply ships, transport ships, and gunboats, and easily captured Yankee supply trains, depots, and garrisons. In making life miserable for the enemy at every turn, he dispirited the Yanks while bolstering Southern enthusiasm.

> Forrest and his men were well-known for their efficient methods of destruction and carnage.

What galled U.S. troops the most was Forrest's November 4-5, 1864, capture and destruction of $6,700,000 ($150 million in today's currency) worth of Federal machinery, along with a gunboat fleet at Johnsonville, Tennessee. Yankee commanders, like Grant, who was driven to "fits of anger" over Forrest's tactics, were both shocked and impressed. But "the Butcher" should have been used to all of this by then: two years earlier, in December 1862, Forrest had incapacitated sixty miles of railroad track connecting Holly Springs, Mississippi, with Columbia, Kentucky, forcing the cigar-chomping Union general to withdraw in despair and disgrace.

Forrest loses another horse, one of twenty-nine that would be shot out from under him during battle. (Image © Lochlainn Seabrook)

THE TENNESSEE CAMPAIGN

THE BATTLE OF SPRING HILL

ON NOVEMBER 29, 1864, THE Confederate soldier-celebrity was at the Battle of Spring Hill, killing Yanks under Rebel General John Bell Hood, chief commander of the Army of Tennessee. He had already butted heads with Hood, who had suffered a number of serious war wounds by then. With one leg gone and a paralyzed arm in a sling, the old-fashioned officer had to be lifted and strapped into his saddle.

It was here, at Spring Hill, Tennessee, that Hood allowed some 25,000 Union soldiers to slip past his Confederate forces in the dead of night. A glaring and tragic military blunder by any definition, it gave the Yanks a full day's head start on the Rebs, allowing them to thoroughly secure themselves in downtown Franklin the next day.

It is impossible to overstate what this one mistake cost the South. Had Hood posted guards the night of the 29th, the Battle of Franklin II could have been avoided the following day. Thousands of lives would have been spared (on both sides), and Nashville would have probably been successfully recaptured by the Confederates two weeks later. Instead, Hood's oversight at Spring Hill literally promised to destroy the Confederacy in the Western Theater. And it did.

THE BATTLE OF FRANKLIN II
The next morning, November 30, Hood called a breakfast meeting at Rippavilla Plantation and, as usual, blamed his subordinates for the

debacle. Forrest, understandably, was outraged and stormed out of the house, with Hood close behind. On the front porch Forrest turned to his handicapped superior and growled: "Sir, if you was a whole man, I'd whip you to within an inch of yer life!"

Forrest then rode with his men up Columbia Pike north into Franklin, where he stood on the rear upper porch of the mansion house at Carnton Plantation to survey the battlefield. He did not like what he saw: several square miles of flat open field known as the Plain of Franklin.

> During the Tennessee Campaign of the Winter of 1864, Forrest's superior, General John Bell Hood, disregarded all of the cavalryman's brilliant suggestions. The result was one disaster after another, all which helped destroy the Confederacy in the Western Theater and ultimately lead the Confederacy down to defeat.

Back at Hood's observation post on Winstead Hill, Forrest once again quarreled with his commander. This time it was about Hood's suicidal plan of attack, which would send some 25,000 Confederate soldiers unprotected across the Plain in full view of a well entrenched enemy. Forrest, like all of the other officers, preferred a flanking maneuver. The perfectly exposed battlefield was quickly dubbed the "Valley of Death" by Hood's pessimistic staff members.

The hardheaded Hood not only ignored Forrest's protestations, but he disregarded the prudent attack strategies of another one of the Army of Tennessee's brilliant cavalrymen, "Stonewall of the West," the Irish General Patrick R. Cleburne, who had suggested moving forward in lifesaving columns rather than in death defying rows. Disgusted with Hood, the Celtic officer turned to his troops and said: "If we are to die, let us die like men." Cleburne's words could not have been more prophetic.

For his "insubordination," an angry Hood sent Cleburne and his men onto the battlefield where the heaviest fighting promised to take place. This would prove to be a momentous decision for both men. Forrest, no doubt, would have been sent into the same area except that his cavalry was desperately needed on the far right, and thus he was spared the fate of Cleburne.

That day, in "five tragic hours," as the Battle of Franklin II has been called, the South lost nearly 2,000 lives, including Cleburne himself, five other generals, and the injury or death of fifty-six regimental commanders. Many thousands more were wounded, lost, or captured. Forrest survived, but the Confederacy never recovered from this terrible blow.

THE BATTLE OF NASHVILLE
The valiant but old school Hood would go on to make a number of other spectactularly poor decisions—sealing the Confederacy's fate in the West. One of these included detaching Forrest to Murfreesboro while he rode on to the Battle of Nashville (December 15-16, 1864) without his most enterprising and sharp-witted officer. Hood not only lost his last battle (and suffered another 4,500 casualties), but he and his men were forced into a tumultuous run for their lives back south toward Franklin.

Despite Hood's poor treatment of Forrest, the intrepid Tennessean managed to save his superior one last time. During "Hood's Retreat" southward, Forrest met up with him at Columbia, Tennessee. Here he rescued what was left of Hood's dilapidated forces from complete annihilation by protecting the army's rear from attack as it was chased from Nashville all the way to Tupelo, Mississippi. Credited with "saving General Hood's army from utter destruction," as an article in *Harper's Weekly* put it, the plucky Confederate officer's impressive tactics earned him another promotion (his last), this time to lieutenant general—one rank shy of full general.

HOOD'S INGLORIOUS FATE
Hood, meanwhile, resigned in dishonor, and the tattered remains of the Army of Tennessee were turned over to General Richard Taylor, the son of America's twelfth president, Zachary Taylor. Hood retired to New Orleans, where he went bankrupt and died, along with his young wife

> General Hood is still blamed by many for the Confederacy's loss in the War for Southern Independence.

Anna Marie Hennen, of the yellow fever epidemic that swept through the city in 1879.

To this day, many have wondered what the outcome of the War for Southern Independence would have been had Forrest been given Hood's position as commander of the Army of Tennessee. Certainly Forrest would have never let Sherman take Atlanta, as Hood did, and thus Lincoln would not have been reelected. It was, after all, Lincoln's election to a second term that sealed the fate of the Confederacy.

Confederate Colonel Edmund Winchester Rucker, a close cousin of the author, led Rucker's Brigade in General Forrest's cavalry. Rucker lost his left arm at the Battle of Nashville, December 15-16, 1864. After the War the two went into the railroad business together for several years (1869-1874). Rucker was the grandson of James Rucker, a cofounder of Memphis, Tennessee. (Image © Lochlainn Seabrook)

President Andrew Johnson "pardoned" Forrest for "treason" against the U.S. on June 17, 1868, a bittersweet victory for the proud and honorable Southerner who had never done anything to threaten the United States or her people. (Image © Lochlainn Seabrook)

THE END OF LINCOLN'S WAR

CONFEDERATE SURRENDER AT APPOMATTOX

IN EARLY APRIL 1865, FORREST was in Alabama hurling himself against Federal troops with his usual ferocity when the doleful message came by telegraph: on April 9 Robert E. Lee had surrendered at Appomattox. It was all over. At least for everyone but Nathan Bedford Forrest.

Though the War had come to an end, Forrest, a natural born warrior who loved the manly, open air life of Johnny Reb, could not bear to put his weapons down. There was something in him that could not accept defeat or offer capitulation, and for a few days he may have, in vain hope, considered the story of Lee's surrender nothing more than a vile Yankee rumor. An April 25th general order to his men would seem to suggest as much:

> "The enemy have originated and sent through our lines various and conflicting dispatches indicating the surrender of General Robert E. Lee and the Army of Virginia. . . . Your commanding general desires to say to you that no credence should be given to such reports. . . . he further assures you that at this time, above all others, it is the duty of every man to stand firm at his post and true to his colors."

With hearsay and confused communications abounding, and with thousands of Confederates across the South, particularly in always independent Texas, refusing to surrender, Forrest's position is not surprising. Even his own troops wanted to continue the fight, though further west, with the Trans-Mississippi Department.

Forrest was sorely tempted; that is, until he heard more bad news. This time it was General Joseph E. Johnston's surrender to Sherman on April 26, at the Bennet House, near Durham Station, North Carolina. Then, a few days later, on April 29, Forrest learned of Taylor's surrender to Union General Edward R. S. Canby, near Mobile, Alabama.

The old battle-scarred fighter could no longer ignore the obvious.

The North had won by simple attrition, over a four-year period grinding down the South with nothing more than superior numbers in men and weaponry. Above all, Lincoln had time on his side: with nearly unlimited financial backing from his Wall Street Boys—whose main profits came from the Yankee slave trade—the U.S. could wage war indefinitely.

> The North only won Lincoln's War by sheer perseverance. Afterward, Grant wrote in his memoirs that if the Confederacy had followed Forrest's plan to simply keep wearing down the North for one more year, the Union would have given up and the South would have been the victor!

While the South, defending her homeland and principles, had fought with far more intensity and determination, in the long term she was unable to sustain herself against such odds. Besides, the always merciful Lee simply could not tolerate seeing his men go one more day barefoot, freezing, and starving. Father Time, Union slave money, and Confederate compassion had, for now, crushed the Southern Cause: constitutional liberty.

Despite the surrender of Lee and Johnston, and the entirely hopeless situation across Dixie, Ol' Bedford continued to roam the now nearly empty battlefields with his men for several months. The North could not rest easy as long as "that Devil Forrest" was on the prowl. It was only a final and definitive "summons to surrender," sent to Forrest from U.S. Brigadier General Edward Hatch on May 3, 1865, that persuaded the diehard commander to finally hang up his famous Navy Sixes.

In Gainesville, Alabama, on May 9, Forrest bid farewell to his men in one of the War's most sublime speeches:

> HEADQUARTERS FORREST'S CAVALRY CORPS,
> GAINESVILLE, ALA., MAY 9, 1865.
>
> "SOLDIERS, By an agreement made between Lieutenant-General Taylor, commanding the Department of Alabama, Mississippi, and East Louisiana, and Major-General Canby, commanding United States forces, the troops of this department have been surrendered.
>
> "I do not think it proper or necessary at this time to refer to causes which have reduced us to this extremity; nor is it now a matter of material consequence to us how such results were brought about. That we are beaten is a self-evident fact, and any further resistance on our part would justly be regarded as the very height of folly and rashness.
>
> "The armies of Generals Lee and Johnston having surrendered, you are the last of all the troops of the Confederate States Army east of the Mississippi River to lay down your arms.
>
> "The Cause for which you have so long and so manfully struggled, and for which you have braved dangers, endured privations, and sufferings, and made so many sacrifices, is today hopeless. The government which we sought to establish and perpetuate, is at an end. Reason dictates and humanity demands that no more blood be shed. Fully realizing and feeling that such is the case, it is your duty and mine to lay down our arms, submit to the 'powers that be,' and to aid in restoring peace and establishing law and order throughout the land.
>
> "The terms upon which you were surrendered are favorable, and should be satisfactory and acceptable to all. They manifest a spirit of magnanimity and liberality, on the part of the Federal authorities, which should be met, on our part, by a faithful compliance with all the stipulations and conditions therein expressed. As your Commander, I sincerely hope that every officer and soldier of my command will cheerfully obey the orders given, and carry out in good faith all the terms of the cartel.
>
> "Those who neglect the terms and refuse to be paroled, may assuredly expect, when arrested, to be sent North and imprisoned. Let those who are absent from their commands, from whatever cause, report at once to this place, or to Jackson, Mississippi; or, if too remote from either, to the nearest United States post or garrison, for parole.
>
> "Civil war, such as you have just passed through naturally engenders feelings of animosity, hatred, and revenge. It is our duty

to divest ourselves of all such feelings; and as far as it is in our power to do so, to cultivate friendly feelings towards those with whom we have so long contended, and heretofore so widely, but honestly, differed. Neighborhood feuds, personal animosities, and private differences should be blotted out; and, when you return home, a manly, straightforward course of conduct will secure the respect of your enemies. Whatever your responsibilities may be to Government, to society, or to individuals, meet them like men.

"The attempt made to establish a separate and independent Confederation has failed; but the consciousness of having done your duty faithfully, and to the end, will, in some measure, repay for the hardships you have undergone.

"In bidding you farewell, rest assured that you carry with you my best wishes for your future welfare and happiness. Without, in any way, referring to the merits of the Cause in which we have been engaged, your courage and determination, as exhibited on many hard-fought fields, has elicited the respect and admiration of friend and foe. And I now cheerfully and gratefully acknowledge my indebtedness to the officers and men of my command whose zeal, fidelity and unflinching bravery have been the great source of my past success in arms.

"I have never, on the field of battle, sent you where I was unwilling to go myself; nor would I now advise you to a course which I felt myself unwilling to pursue. You have been good soldiers, you can be good citizens. Obey the laws, preserve your honor, and the Government to which you have surrendered can afford to be, and will be, magnanimous."

General Forrest after Lincoln's War.
(Image © Lochlainn Seabrook)

FORREST POSTBELLUM

FORREST BEGINS REBUILDING HIS LIFE

FORREST'S DAZZLING MILITARY CAREER WAS at an end and he reentered the civilian world. But any plans he may have had of returning to the role of an ordinary citizen would be short-lived. Life was about to become even more dramatic and controversial for the forty-four year old.

Tragically, as occurred with so many Southern millionaires, the War bankrupted Forrest. Nearly penniless, middle aged, war weary, and suffering from serious wounds, he faced the daunting and nearly incomprehensible task of starting his life over. The word "discouragement" was not in his vocabulary, however.

Moving back to Mississippi, he took up operating a plantation with his new business partner: a former Federal officer. After renting farmland to several other Yankees, Forrest returned to Memphis where he took up residence in a home on the Mississippi River. Here, he settled into the more predictable life of husband and townsman, becoming the president of the Selma, Marion, and Memphis Railroad.

START OF THE KU KLUX KLAN

It is commonly asserted that around this time, in late 1865 or early 1866, Forrest founded the KKK and became its first leader. This fallacy has been in existence for so long that it is now accepted as fact, not only by many of his modern relatives, but also by countless Civil War scholars. Let us briefly examine the history of the group and learn the truth.

The Klan's original mission was simply to maintain law and order throughout the Confederate states during the postwar chaos. Packs of scallywags (Southern opportunists) and carpetbaggers (Northern opportunists), along with gangs of freed former slaves, were roaming the countryside, bribing, intimidating, robbing, and even raping, torturing and killing, members of former Confederate families. Thousands of homes were burned down and countless farms, businesses, and lives were lost.

Amidst the smouldering rubble, armed U.S. forces stalked the streets of what was left of Southern towns, enforcing violent military rule upon an already humiliated and subjugated people. Lincoln's unconstitutional invasion had destroyed much of the South's infrastructure, and so military and legal domination was deemed necessary by arrogant Northern authorities. As part of this monstrous plan, the South, so gloating Yankees believed, would now need to be "reconstructed." And so began twelve additional years (1865-1877) of horror, degradation, and sorrow across Dixie, a period I call "America's Reconstruction Holocaust."

As part of the North's ongoing "reign of terror," illiterate freed slaves were enfranchised—though only if they agreed to cast their vote for the Republican (i.e., the Liberal) ticket, while this same right was denied former Rebel soldiers and their families, intentionally setting the stage for continuing civil and social unrest between blacks and their former owners.

Though big government Liberal Abraham Lincoln was by now dead and gone (assassinated April 14 by John Wilkes Booth, a disillusioned Copperhead), his party's unreasonably harsh and inhumane "Reconstruction" policies remained. These aided in the ongoing debasement of Dixie by treating white Southerners as vanquished foreigners in their own land, and even allowed extreme South-hating

> Pro-North advocates continue to spread numerous lies about Forrest, two of the most absurd being that he started the KKK and was its first leader. There is absolutely no evidence for such claims.

Yanks to illegally push through the Fourteenth Amendment at gunpoint.

In was in this climate of sectional bitterness, panic, frustration, and defeatism that the Ku Klux Klan was born in an effort to protect its own. Not just white Southerners, but black Southerners as well. This is why there were thousands of black members in the original KKK, and why an all-black chapter of the Ku Klux Klan sprang up in Nashville. This was, after all, an anti-Yankee society, not an anti-black one—as uneducated pro-North writers continue to claim.

FORREST'S TRUE ROLE IN THE KKK

Forrest, like so many of his neighbors, was quick to support the fledgling organization, which immediately set up "dens" in various Tennessee towns such as Franklin, Columbia, Shelbyville, and Nashville. With their homes, livelihoods, lives, and very culture at stake, Forrest's decision is not difficult to understand, especially from a 21st-Century perspective. Who today would not want to do all they could to protect the innocent, the weak, the elderly, the widowed, and the orphaned under the same circumstances?

Forrest's support and fame further enhanced the reputation of the Klan and in 1867, at the Nashville KKK Convention, anti-South historians say that he was made the first Grand Dragon of the Tennessee chapter. Unfortunately for those making this claim, indisputable evidence does not exist, for the group kept no written records.

It is my belief that Forrest probably served as some sort of advisor or recruiter. But even this is not known for sure. Forrest himself later denied even being a member, which correlates with what his close friends stated: the General, by then a major Southern celebrity who was considered a "prisoner on parole" by the U.S. government, was too shrewd to become directly involved in a largely covert movement that was under round-the-clock surveillance by his enemies in the North.

Who then was the first Grand Wizard? It was my cousin, former Confederate General George W. Gordon who served in the position from 1865 to 1869, as Gordon's own wife later testified. As for the actual founders, their names are well-known: J. Calvin Jones, Captain John C. Lester, Richard R. Reed, Captain James R. Crowe, Frank O. McCord, and Captain John B. Kennedy created the KKK on Christmas Eve 1865, in a haunted house in Pulaski, Tennessee. Forrest did not even hear about the organization until 1867, two years later.

FORREST ACQUITTED BY THE U.S. GOVERNMENT
Sadly, the same people who promote the lie that Forrest founded and led the KKK refuse to give him credit for something that he actually was responsible for: closing the organization down in 1869.

> The U.S. government investigated Forrest's role in the KKK and found him guiltless. Why then do Forrest's critics continue to link him to the organization?

They also ignore the conspicuous fact that after the War Forrest was ruthlessly scrutinized on the witness stand by a hostile U.S. government investigative committee, which found him completely innocent of any misconduct associated with the organization.

For those with a reasoning mind, these facts alone end any and all disputes concerning Forrest and his relationship with the Klan.

Forrest's men in hand-to-hand combat with the Yankee invader.
(Image © Lochlainn Seabrook)

FORREST'S FINAL YEARS

REPENTANCE, CONVERSION, & BLACK EQUAL RIGHTS

AS FORREST ENTERED THE AUTUMN of his life, he continued to grow and mature, eventually experiencing the sting of regret for past mistakes and sins. Much to his wife Mary Ann's joy, he converted to Christianity, repented, and apologized to those he had wronged.

He also dropped all of his lawsuits (even though his attorneys assured him that they were winnable), and became an ardent civil rights advocate, fighting for black equality. As President of the Selma, Marion, and Memphis Railroad, the one-time states' rights Rebel hired former slaves to work as conductors, engineers, foremen, and architects—jobs still forbidden to blacks in the North at the time.

Nowhere is Forrest's racial philanthropy more evident than in a speech he gave in Memphis on July 4, 1875, to the "Jubilee of Pole Bearers," a sociopolitical group of black Southerners who served as the forerunners of the modern NAACP. As reported by the *Memphis Daily Avalanche*, July 6, 1875:

> After accepting a bouquet of flowers from a member, an African-American woman named Miss Lou Lewis, "as a token, of reconciliation, an offering of peace and good will," the general bowed and replied to the crowd:
> "Miss Lewis, ladies and gentlemen, I accept these flowers as a token of reconciliation between the white and colored races of

the South. I accept them more particularly, since they come from a lady, for if there is any one on God's great earth who loves the ladies, it is myself. This is a proud day for me. Having occupied the position I have for thirteen years, and being misunderstood by the colored race, I take this occasion to say that I am your friend. I am here as the representative of the Southern people—one that has been more maligned than any other. I assure you that every man who was in the Confederate army is your friend. We were born on same soil, breathe the same air, live in the same land, and why should we not be brothers and sisters?

"When the war broke out I believed it to be my duty to fight for my country, and I did so. I came here with the jeers and sneers of a few white people, who did not think it right. I think it is right, and will do all I can to bring about harmony, peace and unity. I want to elevate every man, and to see you take your places in your shops, stores and but I want you to do as I do—go to the polls and select the best men to vote for. I feel that you are free men, I am a free man, and we can do as we please. I came here as a friend and whenever I can serve any of you I will do so. We have one Union, one flag, one country; therefore, let us stand together. Although we differ in color, we should not differ in sentiment. Many things have been said in regard to myself, and many reports circulated, which may perhaps be believed by some of you, but there are many around me who can contradict them. I have been many times in the heat of battle—oftener, perhaps, than any within the sound of my voice. Men have come to me to ask for quarter, both black and white, and I have shielded them. Do your duty as citizens, and if any are oppressed, I will be your friend. I thank you for the flowers, and assure you that I am with you in heart and hand."

FINAL YEARS & DEATH

In his last years Forrest gave generously to charities, in particular those dedicated to Confederate veterans, widows, and orphans, donating, in fact, most of his estate to them. He approved his official biography (by Thomas Jordan and John P. Pryor), and even offered his military services to his old foe Sherman (who flattered him but turned him down).

Frail and emaciated, but still possessing his "blazing eyes" and his fiery Anglo-Celtic spirit, the mellowed, silver-haired, fifty-six year old Confederate chieftain died due to complications from diabetes and old war wounds on October 29, 1877, at Memphis, Tennessee. The powerful Southern light that burned so brightly for nearly six decades was at last gently extinguished. On the 31st his wife buried his remains at Elmwood Cemetery (in 1904 his body was reinterred in Memphis' Nathan Bedford Forrest Park).

The once headstrong warrior went Home a humbled peacemaker. But not before offering one final glimpse of his true impact on the Victorian South. Of the 10,000 individuals who paid their final respects at Forrest's funeral, 3,000 were African-Americans.

Dressed in black, they mourned right alongside their European-American counterparts. Among those walking in the three mile long cortege were many of the survivors from the General's original slave force from twenty-five years earlier, as well as his sixty-five loyal black Confederate soldiers. Contrast this with black colonizationist Lincoln's funeral, in which African-Americans were banned from attending altogether.

> Completely contrary to Yankee myth, Forrest was a great friend of African-Americans, and spent the latter half of his life campaigning for black civil rights.

General Forrest in his senior years.
(Image © Lochlainn Seabrook)

18

AN "UNTUTORED MILITARY GENIUS"

A ONE-OF-A-KIND SOLDIER

TO THIS DAY NATHAN BEDFORD Forrest is hailed by many as the paragon of Southern manhood and the archetypal Confederate officer by which all other soldiers—past, present, and future—will forever be measured; not just in the U.S., but around the world. Of him General Joseph E. Johnston noted:

> "Had Forrest the advantages of a thorough military education and training he would have been the great central figure of the war."

Truly an "untutored military genius," as he has been called, Forrest is internationally considered the most innovative and outstanding American cavalryman to have ever lived. Indeed, his natural leadership skills, his ability to improvise quickly on the field of action, his seemingly psychic capacity for reading the mind of the enemy, and his intrinsic sense of military tactics, know no equal. All this from a man who, unlike most of his colleagues, possessed no law degree and never attended West Point—or any proper school for that matter.

Forrest, in fact, despised the idea of "fightin' by the rules," and never tried to hide his profound disdain for schooled military men, and in particular "West Pinters," as he referred to them. Whether they were

Yankees or Rebels, it made no difference: he frequently butted heads with both. Still, he held special contempt for Union West Pointers. After trouncing dozens of them in battle, the wholly untrained military man had this to say on the subject:

> "Whenever I met one of them fellers that fit by note, I generally whipped hell out of him before he got his tune pitched."

UNCONVENTIONAL CAVALRYMAN

Forrest's unorthodox military habits alone could fill a large volume. Among them were the unrestrained recklessness with which he approached battle, his near-total disregard for following the orders of his superiors, and the sharpening of his saber to a razor's edge and wearing it on his right side. During the War he also grew and wore his hair long, stood in his stirrups as he rode, and refused to use field glasses (binoculars), preferring the naked eye for observation, even over great distances.

> Forrest's military skills, unlike nearly every other Confederate officer, were self-taught. Indeed, he was one of the few Rebel generals who did not attend West Point—a fact he was very proud of!

An enthusiast of lightning fast surprise attacks and dashing offensive maneuvers (such as quickly and violently cutting off an enemy's rearguard), Forrest introduced the "hit-and-run" guerilla tactic, still employed by modern armies. A master of the double-flanking maneuver (his spirited yell, "hit 'em on the end boys," was well-known to his troops), he also promoted the use of the mounted saber assault, as well as the "raiding" approach while maneuvering against the enemy. His cavalry might have been more aptly called a dismounted infantry, since he normally deployed his troops on foot, using his horses mainly for rapid transport.

MILITARY SKILLS

The General's "calling card" was elegant in its simplicity: he always did what the enemy least expected. This usually involved galloping at full speed into the heart of the battle, where he and his company of prize soldiers, "Forrest's Escort," would surround the enemy before it could react, unmercifully hit their flanks and rear, call their bluff (by greatly exaggerating the number of his troops and artillery), then offer the famed Forrest surrender-or-die "truce." Few Yankee officers dared refuse the Confederate General's generous but bone-chilling offer to relinquish their weapons "in order to prevent the further effusion of blood." Those who did, *and* lived to tell about it, always regretted it!

A highly skilled swordsman who, against army regulations, sharpened both the top and the bottom edges of his sabers (to expedite the dispatch of the enemy), Forrest also helped develop the idea of mobile warfare. Here, an army is relentlessly chased, harassed, and attacked until it either surrenders or is killed off. One-hundred fifty years later, these and dozens of other tactics and techniques invented or refined by Forrest are still being studied at military schools around the world.

General Forrest's beautiful equestrian statue at Memphis, Tennessee. (Image © Lochlainn Seabrook)

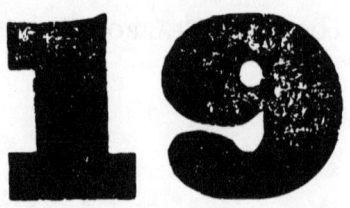

A BLUFF BEATS A STREIGHT

FORREST & A CONFEDERATE HEROINE

AN OUTSTANDING EXAMPLE OF FORREST'S use of mobile warfare occurred during his clash with Union General Abel Streight, a fight that Forrest was assisted in by a young patriotic Confederate girl.

On April 29, 1863, hearing from his scouts that Streight was nearby, Forrest and his men hurried out of the town of Courtland, Lawrence County, Alabama, in a bitter rain. On April 30, at Day's Gap, Forrest caught up with Streight's rearguard and a battle ensued. Forrest gave his usual order: "Shoot at everythin' blue, and keep up the skeer!" Streight managed to repel the Confederates long enough to get away. But, vastly underestimating his wily pursuer, the Union officer did not realize that in reality there was no escape from Forrest.

The unyielding Rebel officer nipped at Streight's heels almost unceasingly for several more days, engaging the Yanks in numerous skirmishes, gradually wearing them down.

On May 2, at Black Creek, on the road between Blountsville and Gadsden, Forrest found that Streight had crossed the only bridge in the area and burned it behind him. While the General was pondering his next move, he came upon a young Confederate girl, Emma Sansom, who told him of a shallow "lost ford" downstream. With no time to lose, Forrest pulled the youngster up onto his saddle and sped away with her guiding him.

> Like Forrest himself, Emma Sansom was a true Confederate hero. That's her on the cover of this book, in John Paul Strain's wonderful painting of the May 2, 1863, incident. Emma is riding behind General Forrest, leading him "to the lost ford." For her help, Forrest gave Emma a horse, and later, after the War, the governor of Alabama presented her with land and a gold medal for her bravery.

Locating the crossing amid a hail of Yankee bullets from across the river, the Southern celebrity quickly took Emma home and dropped her safely off with her starstruck mother. Emma's brave assistance saved Forrest at least three hours, valuable time that brought him to within breathing distance of the enemy, unbeknownst to Streight.

Horrified to discover Forrest now just behind him, Streight and his troops rode "like the wind," but all for nought. Because of Forrest's relentless pursuit, the Yanks and their horses had not eaten or slept for several days, eventually running out of steam. After Forrest tricked Streight into believing that he possessed far more men and artillery than he actually had, the exhausted and humiliated Federals finally gave up near Cedar Bluff, Alabama, on May 3, 1863.

Forrest had marched and fought for five days and nights, traversing 135 miles of mountainous terrain nearly nonstop, capturing an entire U.S. command nearly three times the size of his own. Classic Forrest.

Emma Sansom, Confederate heroine and a cousin of the author—who descends from the Sansoms. (Image © Lochlainn Seabrook)

"NATURE'S SOLDIER"

THE CONFEDERATE CONGRESS THANKS FORREST

HERE WE HAVE THE EMBODIMENT of the "shock and awe" approach to fighting, used today by America's modern military. Forrest, ahead of his time, was employing this maneuver a century and a half ago.

For his valor that Spring, the Confederate Congress personally thanked him for "the daring, skill, and perseverance exhibited in the pursuit and capture of the largely superior forces of the enemy" (this was only one of four official congressional "thanks" Forrest would receive during the War). His capture of Streight has rightly been called "one of the most remarkable performances known to warfare."

AN UNAPPRECIATED VIRTUOSO

Unfortunately, the genius behind such feats was not fully recognized by Forrest's superiors until it was too late, as the postbellum writings of President Jefferson Davis and General Robert E. Lee attest. We can be sure of one thing: had Forrest been placed at the head of the Army of Tennessee early on, the Confederate States of America would be alive and well today, and 120 million Southerners would be living in peace, freedom, and prosperity.

Strange that, at the time, U.S. officers seem to have appreciated Forrest's brilliance more than his own commanders. Sherman, for instance, called Forrest "the most remarkable man our Civil War produced," a sentiment echoed by thousands of professional soldiers into the present day. Of Forrest's talents on the battlefield, Sherman wrote:

> "He had a genius which was to me incomprehensible. . . . He always seemed to know what I was doing or intended to do, while I am free to confess I could never tell or form any satisfactory idea of what he was trying to accomplish."

"WAR MEANS KILLIN'"

From childhood, Forrest was as "comfortable as a Comanche" on horseback, a trait for which he was nicknamed the "Wizard of the Saddle." The only individual—Confederate or Union—to rise from private to lieutenant general during the War, he never lost a battle in which he was chief commander (until his last at Selma); twenty-nine horses were shot out from under him; he himself was shot at 179 times; he killed thirty-one Union soldiers and wounded hundreds more; he destroyed or seized tens of millions of dollars of Yankee supplies; and finally, he captured some 31,000 prisoners. Impressive statistics for a military man from any time period.

> Forrest broke many records and achieved many firsts during Lincoln's War. Confederate General Richard Taylor compared Forrest to the author's cousin, the great English warrior and military leader, King Richard the Lion-Hearted!

How did he do it? Forrest's combat formula was rudimentary but highly effective. As he himself stated:

> "War means killin', and the way to kill is to get thar' first with the most men."

"NATURE'S SOLDIER"

So highly venerated is Forrest today among those who know the real man that his very name is synonymous with heroism, genius, and inventiveness. Of him Lord Garnet Joseph Wolseley, Commander-in-Chief of the British Army, said:

"Panic found no resting place in that calm brain of his, and no danger, no risk, appalled that dauntless spirit. Inspired with true military instincts, he was verily nature's soldier."

Little wonder that Southern children, pets, cars, trucks, streets, schools, local parks, State parks, cemeteries, businesses, golf courses, apartment complexes, libraries, office buildings, and subdivisions are still named after him, or that author Winston Groom named the lead character in his film "Forrest Gump" after the temerarious frontiersman.

An example of Forrest's handwriting, from a September 21, 1863, dispatch addressed to Confederate General Leonidas Polk. It was written while "on the road." (Image © Lochlainn Seabrook)

A HERO FOR THE AGES

SOUTHERN CHAMPION, AMERICAN PARAGON

THOSE WHO DENOUNCE FORREST HAVE been indoctrinated by Northern myth. The fact is that his amazing rags-to-riches story epitomizes the American Dream. Consider the following: against nearly insurmountable odds, he rose above the limitations of dire indigence, disease, and a large fatherless family to become a self-made millionaire, and one of the most prosperous men in the U.S., all before the age of forty.

Along the way, the self-taught individualist literally pulled himself up by his own boot straps, transforming himself from an impoverished, impulsive rustic, into a wealthy, sophisticated humanitarian, all with less than six months of formal education.

After giving four years of his life to the War for Southern Independence, he managed to survive serious war wounds, criticism, slander, and bankruptcy. He then built his fortunes back up again through hard work, determination, and sheer grit, in spite of a large coterie of bigots arrayed against him.

In a state where whiskey and tobacco were king, he eschewed both alcohol and smoking. And though his temper, cursing, and gambling sometimes got the best of him, the fearless cavalryman eventually subdued all three, channeling his reckless energies into more constructive social and spiritual pursuits.

Forrest had many admirable traits. Among them were gumption, drive, ambition, perseverance, and the refusal to accept defeat. He never gave in when he believed he was in the right, and was known to approach desperate situations with a cool and calculating head. Never a quitter, he always finished what he started, no matter how difficult the road ahead. An innate leader, he inspired and motivated all those around him, often even his enemies, with his composed but forceful presence. And yet this formidable mountaineer, who considered himself the personal protector of women and children, was capable of the deepest sympathy, mercifulness, and tenderness.

> The only people who dislike Forrest are the ones who do not know the real man. They accept Yankee lies, slander, and mythology over the facts.

A seemingly simple man outwardly, he was actually an exceptionally complex person whose thoughtful and calm exterior hid an indefatigable physical energy and a mercurial mind that was always on the go. Indeed, Forrest never seemed to grow tired and seldom slept. As one of his officers said of him, he was, in fact, "more like that of a piece of powerful steam machinery than a human being."

THE BLACK MAN'S FRIEND
Raised in a Eurocentric America where Northerners often viewed African slaves as little more than human livestock, Southerner Forrest instead saw them as people, invaluable servants to be treated humanely and respectfully. Incorrectly known by the anti-South movement as a "lifelong slaver," he was actually only in the business a short time: he was a slave owner for just eleven years (from 1852 to 1863), while he was in the slave trading business for a mere seven years (from 1852 to 1859). This is quite in contrast to Yankees like Ulysses S. Grant, who was involved in slavery for decades, before, during, and after the War.

Indeed, after closing down his slave trading business two years before Lincoln's unlawful invasion, Forrest emancipated or sold most of his slaves, then took the rest into the Confederate army with him, where he integrated them directly into his command—selecting seven to serve as his personal armed guard. He had promised these forty-five servants their freedom at war's end, but instead emancipated them in September 1863, shortly following the Battle of Chickamauga.

After the "late unpleasantness," he happily hired back many of his former black servants, now as regular employees, and fought for racial equality, stating: "There is no need for a war of races. I want to see the whole country prosper." As the head of numerous postbellum businesses, he promoted the idea of repopulating the South with more Africans, then hired blacks for a wide variety of jobs (many of them quite technical)—a violation of the North's racist Black Codes.

THE GENERAL'S FUNNY BONE
Though many think of "Ol' Bedford" as a grave and solemn figure, in truth he loved a good chuckle and had a wonderful, lively sense of humor, as the following wartime story reveals.

One rainy day in the Fall of 1864, not far from Tullahoma, Tennessee, Forrest spied a Rebel soldier struggling to move a captured caisson (an ammunition chest) stuck fast in the mud. The always efficiency-minded Forrest assumed the man was not applying himself to the task properly. Riding up to the unwitting trooper, the General yelled: "Who's in charge here?"

"I am sir. Captain Andrew McGregor!" came the crisp reply from the sharply saluting officer.

Unruffled by this response, Forrest barked: "Then why in the hell don't you do somethin' about that thar' chest? Move that goddamned piece of equipment. Now!"

McGregor jumped up and shouted: "I shall not be cursed out by anyone, even a superior officer!" With that, he spitefully grabbed a lit torch, opened the caisson lid, and thrust the fiery brand inside.

Now this was a sight that would horrify even the most jaded soldier, and Forrest was no exception. Putting spurs to his horse, he let out a string of profanities, along with a loud warning to others to vacate the area immediately.

Arriving out of breath at camp, he inquired of his staff: "Who the hell is that lunatic down thar'? He just tried to blow the two of us up with a caisson full of powder!"

Knowing the box was empty, his men let out a hearty laugh; and so did Forrest—once he realized the joke was on him. However, after that it was observed that the General never swore at Captain McGregor again.

A MAN OF KINDNESS & INTEGRITY

During the War, Yankee General James H. Wilson happened to meet Forrest during a truce. Like so many others, Wilson came away from this brief and unexpected encounter with nothing but awe and admiration for the rough-hewn Southern gentleman. According to Wilson, as he and his men were about to depart Forrest's camp, "the General took my hand in his own . . . and holding it in a cordial grasp, said in a friendly and courteous manner: 'From now on, don't git too far away from your command when you come down into this country sah—some of our boys may pick you up.'"

> Though a tough Tennessee mountaineer, a shrewd and powerful multimillionaire, and an aggressive and unrelenting soldier, Forrest was also a kindhearted man who defended women and children, gave generously to charities, and always placed the welfare of others over his own.

Forrest was also a good and trusted friend to all who knew him. This despite being betrayed, taken advantage of, and verbally and even physically attacked on numerous occasions. And for his role in trying to preserve Southern law and order, Southern culture, and Southern pride during the horrors of "Reconstruction," he became forever acknowledged as the "Spiritual Comforter" of the Southern people, a title which he carries across Dixie to this day.

MILITARY MAN EXTRAORDINAIRE

Then there is Forrest's military record, which is nothing short of astonishing; especially considering his early life as an unschooled farm boy. And though his independent spirit and brashness sometimes prevented promotion, on the field of action his great natural intelligence and absolute fearlessness awed both his superiors and his enemies. Not only this, but his love and respect for his troops inspired thousands to fight faithfully for the Southern Cause under his stouthearted leadership. Many would echo the words of a Confederate officer who once said: "Forrest's capacity for war seemed only to be limited by the opportunities for its display."

GENEROUS FAMILY MAN
Forrest proved to be an excellent father and an industrious provider, as well as a faithful, lifelong husband (unlike the vast majority of men then as today, he only married once), and up until his death at age fifty-six, he gave generously to both family members and charities.

Forrest with his signature. It reads: "N. B. Forrest, Lieut. Genrl." (Image © Lochlainn Seabrook)

RIDIN' WITH FORREST

FORREST'S LAST BATTLE

HIS FINAL AND MOST IMPORTANT engagement took place on his own inner battlefield, where he conquered his greatest foe and was born again, becoming a "new creature in Christ." His life thus reminds us that being a Christian is about mercy, forgiveness, and transformation; in other words, spiritual growth. Is this not the Christian ideal?

> Forrest was a great man and a faithful Southerner, who died too young. If only we had had more Forrests during Lincoln's War. Can there be any doubt that the South would have won? Those who know the true Forrest will always honor his name and memory.

Those who would condemn him would do well to consider the words of the Savior he worshiped (John 8:7). For "that Devil Forrest" turns out to be neither a demon or a deity. Just a man. But not just any man.

RIDIN' WITH FORREST

Nathan Bedford Forrest was a rare American original, an honest-to-God American patriot, and a hellbent-for-leather American hero who helped forge the world's greatest nation out of an untamed wilderness. More importantly to us here in Dixie, he supported and defended the Southern Confederacy, both saving thousands of lives and helping to thwart dictator Lincoln's assault on the Constitution and the Southern people. The General will thus always be a traditional Southern icon, an integral part of our dual American heritage, and a major player on the stage of world history.

By any standard, in any time or place, this makes him an extraordinary person and an inspiring real life role model who deserves to be commended, emulated, and revered. Those of us who have taken the time to truly get to know him understand. We are "ridin' with Forrest"!

Forrest monument at the site of the General's birth, July 13, 1821, at Chapel Hill, Tennessee. The original home disappeared long ago, a victim of time and the elements. The Confederate Battle Flag flies on the left, the Bonnie Blue Flag in on the right. (Image © Lochlainn Seabrook)

THE FORREST HOME FUND

Help Preserve

FORREST'S BOYHOOD HOME

Chapel Hill, Tennessee

(Image © Lochlainn Seabrook)

If you'd like to help maintain this unique historical landmark and aid in the ongoing restoration process and the building of a visitor's center, if you're interested in donating your time, energy, or supplies, or if you or your parents would like to sponsor this project, please mail your correspondence or contribution to:

The Forrest Home Fund
C/O Sons of Confederate Veterans
PO Box 59
Columbia, TN 38402-0059

BIBLIOGRAPHY

Alotta, Robert I. *Civil War Justice: Union Army Executions Under Lincoln.* Shippensburg, PA: White Mane, 1989.
Ashdown Paul, and Edward Caudill. *The Myth of Nathan Bedford Forrest.* 2005. Lanham, MD: Rowman and Littlefield, 2006 ed.
Ashe, Captain Samuel A'Court. *A Southern View of the Invasion of the Southern States and War of 1861-1865.* 1935. Crawfordville, GA: Ruffin Flag Company, 1938 ed.
Bearss, Edwin C. *Forrest at Brice's Cross Roads.* Dayton, OH: Morningside Bookshop, 1979.
Bradley, Michael R. *Nathan Bedford Forrest's Escort and Staff.* Gretna, LA: Pelican Publishing Co., 2006.
Bradshaw, Wayne. *The Civil War Diary of William R. Dyer: A Member of Forrest's Escort.* Charleston, SC: BookSurge, 2009.
Brady, Cyrus Townsend. *Three Daughters of the Confederacy.* New York, NY: G. W. Dillingham, 1905.
Browning, Robert, M., Jr. *Forrest: The Confederacy's Relentless Warrior.* Dulles, VA: Brassey's, Inc., 2004.
Currotto, William F. *Wizard of the Saddle: Nathan Bedford Forrest.* N.p.: Patchwork Books, 1996.
Fisher, John E. *They Rode With Forrest and Wheeler: A Chronicle of Five Tennessee Brothers' Service in the Confederate Western Cavalry.* Jefferson, NC: McFarland and Co., 1995.
Gentry, Claude. *General Nathan Bedford Forrest: The Boy and the Man.* Macon, GA: Magnolia, 1972.
Hafendorfer, Kenneth A. *Nathan Bedford Forrest: The Distant Storm - The Murfreesboro Raid of July 13, 1862.* Louisville, KY: KH Press, 1997.
Henry, Robert Selph. *The Story of the Confederacy.* 1931. New York, NY: Konecky and Konecky, 1999 ed.
———. (ed.). *As They Saw Forrest: Some Recollections and Comments of Contemporaries.* 1956. Wilmington, NC: Broadfoot Publishing Co., 1991 ed.
———. *First with the Most: Forrest.* New York, NY: Konecky and Konecky, 1992.
Hills, Parker. *A Study in Warfighting: Nathan Bedford Forrest and the Battle of Brice's Crossroads.* Saline, MI: McNaughton and Gunn, 1996.
Hurst, Jack. *Nathan Bedford Forrest: A Biography.* 1993. New York, NY: Vintage, 1994 ed.
Jensen, Merrill. *The New Nation: A History of the United States During the Confederation, 1781-1789.* New York, NY: Vintage, 1950.
———. *The Articles of Confederation: An Interpretation of the Social-Constitutional History of the American Revolution, 1774-1781.* Madison, WI: University of Wisconsin Press, 1959.
Jordan, Thomas, and John P. Pryor. *The Campaigns of General Nathan Bedford Forrest and of Forrest's Cavalry.* New Orleans, LA: Blelock and Co., 1868.
Ladnier, Gene. *General Nathan Bedford Forrest on Fame's Eternal Battlefield.* Charleston, SC: BookSurge, 2001.
Lytle, Andrew Nelson. *Bedford Forrest and His Critter Company.* New York, NY: G. P. Putnam's Sons, 1931.
Maness, Lonnie E. *An Untutored Genius: The Military Career of General Nathan Bedford Forrest.* Oxford, MS: Guild Bindery, 1990.
Mathes, Capt. J. Harvey. *General Forrest.* New York, NY: D. Appleton and Co., 1902.
Meriwether, Elizabeth Avery. *Facts and Falsehoods Concerning the War on the South, 1861-1865.* (Originally written under the pseudonym "George Edmonds".) Memphis, TN: A. R. Taylor, 1904.
Morton, John Watson. *The Artillery of Nathan Bedford Forrest's Cavalry.* Nashville, TN: The M. E. Church, 1909.
Neely, Mark E., Jr. *The Fate of Liberty: Abraham Lincoln and Civil Liberties.* New York, NY: Oxford University Press, 1991.

ORA (full title: *The War of the Rebellion: A Compilation of the Official Records of the Union and Confederate Armies*. (Multiple volumes.) Washington, D.C.: Government Printing Office, 1880.
ORN (full title: *Official Records of the Union and Confederate Navies in the War of the Rebellion*). (Multiple volumes.) Washington, D.C.: Government Printing Office, 1894.
Owsley, Frank Lawrence. *King Cotton Diplomacy: Foreign Relations of the Confederate States of America*. 1931. Chicago, IL: University of Chicago Press, 1959 ed.
Parks, Aileen Wells. *Bedford Forrest: Horseback Boy*. 1952. Indianapolis, IN: Bobbs-Merrill Co., 1963 ed.
Phillips, Ulrich Bonnell. *American Negro Slavery: A Survey of the Supply, Employment and Control of Negro Labor as Determined by the Plantation Régime*. New York, NY: D. Appleton and Co., 1929.
Pollard, Edward A. *Southern History of the War*. 2 vols in 1. New York, NY: Charles B. Richardson, 1866.
——. *The Lost Cause*. 1867. Chicago, IL: E. B. Treat, 1890 ed.
——. *Lee and His Lieutenants: Comprising the Early Life, Public Services, and Campaigns of General Robert E. Lee and His Companions in Arms*. New York, NY: E. B. Treat, 1867.
——. *The Lost Cause Regained*. New York, NY: G. W. Carlton and Co., 1868.
——. *Life of Jefferson Davis, With a Secret History of the Southern Confederacy, Gathered "Behind the Scenes in Richmond."* Philadelphia, PA: National Publishing Co., 1869.
Seabrook, Lochlainn. *The Caudills: An Etymological, Ethnological, and Genealogical Study - Exploring the Name and National Origins of a European-American Family*. 2003. Franklin, TN: Sea Raven Press, 2010 ed.
——. *Carnton Plantation Ghost Stories: True Tales of the Unexplained From Tennessee's Most Haunted Civil War House!* 2005. Franklin, TN: Sea Raven Press, 2010 ed.
——. *Nathan Bedford Forrest: Southern Hero, American Patriot: Honoring a Confederate Hero and the Old South*. 2007. Franklin, TN: Sea Raven Press, 2010 ed.
——. *Abraham Lincoln: The Southern View - Demythologizing America's Sixteenth President*. 2007. Franklin, TN: Sea Raven Press, 2013 ed.
——. *The McGavocks of Carnton Plantation: A Southern History - Celebrating One of Dixie's Most Noble Confederate Families and Their Tennessee Home*. 2008. Franklin, TN: Sea Raven Press, 2011 ed.
——. *A Rebel Born: A Defense of Nathan Bedford Forrest, Confederate General, American Legend*. Franklin, TN: Sea Raven Press, 2010.
——. *Everything You Were Taught About the Civil War is Wrong, Ask a Southerner!* 2010. Franklin, TN: Sea Raven Press, 2012 ed.
——. *The Quotable Jefferson Davis: Selections From the Writings and Speeches of the Confederacy's First President*. Franklin, TN: Sea Raven Press, 2011 Sesquicentennial Civil War Edition.
——. *The Quotable Robert E. Lee: Selections From the Writings and Speeches of the South's Most Beloved Civil War General*. Franklin, TN: Sea Raven Press, 2011 Sesquicentennial Civil War Edition.
——. *The Unquotable Abraham Lincoln: The President's Quotes They Don't Want You to Know!* Franklin, TN: Sea Raven Press, 2011 Sesquicentennial Civil War Edition.
——. *The Old Rebel: Robert E. Lee As He Was Seen By His Contemporaries*. Franklin, TN: Sea Raven Press, 2012 Sesquicentennial Civil War Edition.
——. *The Quotable Stonewall Jackson: Selections From the Writings and Speeches of the South's Most Famous General*. Franklin, TN: Sea Raven Press, 2012 Sesquicentennial Civil War Edition.
——. *Lincolnology: The Real Abraham Lincoln Revealed in His Own Words - A Study of Lincoln's Suppressed, Misinterpreted, and Forgotten Writings and Speeches*. Franklin, TN: Sea Raven Press, 2011 Sesquicentennial Civil War Edition.
——. *Honest Jeff and Dishonest Abe: A Southern Children's Guide to the Civil War*. Franklin, TN: Sea Raven Press, 2012 Sesquicentennial Civil War Edition.
——. *Give 'Em Hell Boys! The Complete Military Correspondence of Nathan Bedford Forrest*. Franklin, TN: Sea Raven Press, 2012 Sesquicentennial Civil War Edition.

——. *The Constitution of the Confederate States of America Explained: A Clause-by-Clause Study of the South's Magna Carta.* Franklin, TN: Sea Raven Press, 2012 Sesquicentennial Civil War Edition.
——. *The Great Impersonator! 99 Reasons to Dislike Abraham Lincoln.* Franklin, TN: Sea Raven Press, 2012 Sesquicentennial Civil War Edition.
——. *Forrest! 99 Reasons to Love Nathan Bedford Forrest.* Franklin, TN: Sea Raven Press, 2012 Sesquicentennial Civil War Edition.
——. *The Quotable Nathan Bedford Forrest: Selections From the Writings and Speeches of the Confederacy's Most Brilliant Cavalryman.* Franklin, TN: Sea Raven Press, 2012 Sesquicentennial Civil War Edition.
——. *Encyclopedia of the Battle of Franklin: A Comprehensive Guide to the Conflict That Changed the Civil War.* Franklin, TN: Sea Raven Press, 2012 Sesquicentennial Civil War Edition.
——. *The Alexander H. Stephens Reader: Excerpts From the Works of a Confederate Founding Father.* Franklin, TN: Sea Raven Press, 2013 Sesquicentennial Civil War Edition.
——. *The Quotable Alexander H. Stephens: Selections From the Writings and Speeches of the Confederacy's First Vice President.* Franklin, TN: Sea Raven Press, 2013 Sesquicentennial Civil War Edition.
Sheppard, Eric William. *Bedford Forrest, The Confederacy's Greatest Cavalryman.* 1930. Dayton, OH: Morningside House, 1981 ed.
Starnes, H. Gerald. *Forrest's Forgotten Horse Brigadier.* Westminster, MD: Heritage Books, 1995.
Wallcut, R. F. (pub.). *Southern Hatred of the American Government, the People of the North, and Free Institutions.* Boston, MA: R. F. Wallcut, 1862.
Warner, Ezra J. *Generals in Gray: Lives of the Confederate Commanders.* 1959. Baton Rouge, LA: Louisiana State University Press, 1989 ed.
——. *Generals in Blue: Lives of the Union Commanders.* 1964. Baton Rouge, LA: Louisiana State University Press, 2006 ed.
Wills, Brian Steel. *The Confederacy's Greatest Cavalryman: Nathan Bedford Forrest.* Lawrence, KS: University Press of Kansas, 1992.
Wilson, Clyde N. *Why the South Will Survive: Fifteen Southerners Look at Their Region a Half Century After I'll Take My Stand.* Athens, GA: University of Georgia Press, 1981.
——. (ed.) *The Essential Calhoun: Selections From Writings, Speeches, and Letters.* New Brunswick, NJ: Transaction Publishers, 1991.
——. *A Defender of Southern Conservatism: M.E. Bradford and His Achievements.* Columbia, MO: University of Missouri Press, 1999.
——. *From Union to Empire: Essays in the Jeffersonian Tradition.* Columbia, SC: The Foundation for American Education, 2003.
——. *Defending Dixie: Essays in Southern History and Culture.* Columbia, SC: The Foundation for American Education, 2005.
Witherspoon, William. *Reminiscences of a Scout, Spy and Soldier of Forrest's Cavalry.* Jackson, TN: McCowat Mercer Printing Co., 1910.
Wyeth, John Allan. *Life of General Nathan Bedford Forrest.* New York, NY: Harper and Brothers, 1899.
——. *That Devil Forrest* (redacted modern version of Wyeth's *Life of General Nathan Bedford Forrest*). 1959. Baton Rouge, LA: Louisiana State University Press, 1989 ed.
Young, Bennett Henderson. *Confederate Wizards of the Saddle.* 1914. Lanham, MD: J. S. Sanders and Co., 1999 ed.

INDEX

Anderson, Charles W., 36
Atkins, Chet, 112
Beauregard, Pierre G. T., 112
Beck, Fanny, 21, 26
Beck, Mariam, 16, 21, 24, 26
Bernstein, Leonard, 112
Boone, Pat, 112
Booth, John W., 78
Bragg, Braxton, 53
Brooke, Edward W., 112
Buckner, Simon B., 45, 46, 49, 50
Calloway, Matthew C., 36
Canby, Edward R. S., 73, 74
Carson, Martha, 112
Carter, Theodrick "Tod", 112
Cash, John Carter, 112
Cash, Johnny, 112
Caudill, Benjamin E., 111, 112
Cheairs, Nathaniel F., 112
Chesnut, Mary, 112
Clay, Henry, 38
Cleburne, Patrick R., 68, 69
Cowan, James B., 36
Cowan, Samuel M., 29
Cromwell, James, 112
Crowe, James R., 80
Cruise, Tom, 112
Cyrus, Billy Ray, 112
Cyrus, Miley, 112
Davis, Jefferson, 9, 38, 53, 93
Early, Jubal, 113
Edward I, King, 111
Floyd, John B., 45, 46, 49, 50
Forrest, Francis A., 29
Forrest, Jeffrey, 41, 56
Forrest, Jonathan, 25, 29
Forrest, Nathan, 17

Forrest, Nathan B., 11-18, 21-23, 25-35, 40-47, 49-55, 57-61, 63-70, 72-74, 76-80, 82-84, 86-88, 90, 91, 93, 94, 97-104, 112
Forrest, Thomas, 17
Forrest, William, 16, 18, 21
Forrest, William M., 29, 36, 41
Gist, States Rights, 112
Gordon, George W., 79, 112
Gould, Andrew W., 54
Grant, Ulysses S., 35, 45, 46, 48-50, 52, 60, 65, 73, 98
Graves, Robert, 111
Groom, Winston, 95
Guaraldi, Vince, 112
Gump, Forrest, 95
Halleck, Henry W., 48, 49
Harding, William G., 112
Harris, Isham G., 42
Hatch, Edward, 73
Hennen, Anna M., 70
Hood, John B., 62, 67-70, 112
Houston, Sam, 28
Hubbard, John M., 64
Jackson, Thomas Stonewall, 112
James, Jesse, 112
Jefferson, Thomas, 114
Jent, Elias, Sr., 112
Jesus, 103
John, Elton, 112
Johnson, Andrew, 71
Johnston, Albert S., 47, 52
Johnston, Joseph E., 73, 74, 86
Jones, J. Calvin, 80
Jordan, Thomas, 83
Judd, Ashley, 112

Judd, Naomi, 112
Judd, Wynonna, 112
Kelley, David C., 33
Kennedy, John B., 80
Lee, Robert E., 49, 72-74, 93, 112
Lester, John C., 80
Lewis, Lou, 82
Lincoln, Abraham, 9, 14, 35, 37, 38, 40-42, 47, 53, 54, 60, 70, 73, 78, 84, 94, 98, 103, 112
Longstreet, James, 112
Loveless, Patty, 112
Luxton, Joseph, 24
Madison, Bailee, 112
Matlock, James, 25
Matlock, Jefferson, 25
Matlock, T. J., 25
Maury, Abram P., 112
Mayfield, W. S., 18
McClellan, George B., 48, 49
McCord, Frank O., 80
McGavock, John W., 112
McGraw, Tim, 112
McGregor, Andrew, 99, 100
Montgomery, Elizabeth, 28
Montgomery, Mary Ann, 28, 29, 82
Montgomery, Richard, 28
Morgan, John H., 112
Morton, John W., 36
Mosby, John Singleton, 112
Nelson, Louis N., 55
Nugent, Ted, 112
Oxford, Earl of, 111
Parton, Dolly, 112
Pillow, Gideon J., 45, 46
Polk, Leonidas, 42, 95
Presley, Elvis, 112

Pryor, John P., 83
Rambaut, Gilbert V., 36
Rathbone, Jackson, 112
Reagan, Ronald, 112
Reed, Richard R., 80
Reynolds, Burt, 112
Richard the Lion-Hearted, 94
Robbins, Hargus, 112
Robert the Bruce, King, 111
Rucker, Edmund W., 70, 112
Rucker, James, 70
Sansom, Emma, 90, 92
Scruggs, Earl, 112
Seabrook, John Lawton, 112
Seabrook, Lochlainn, 11, 111, 112, 115
Seger, Bob, 112
Severson, Charles S., 36
Sherman, William T., 11, 44, 60, 63, 70, 73, 83, 93, 94
Skaggs, Ricky, 112
Stephens, Alexander H., 9, 50
Strain, John P., 91, 113, 114
Strange, John P., 36
Streight, Abel, 90, 91, 93
Stuart, Jeb, 112, 113
Sturgis, Samuel D., 63, 64
Taylor, Richard, 69, 74, 94, 112
Taylor, Zachary, 69
White, Josiah S., 41
Wilson, James H., 100
Wilson, Wallace, 24
Winbush, Nelson W., 55
Witherspoon, Reese, 112
Wolseley, Garnet J., 94
Womack, John B., 112
Womack, Lee Ann, 112
Wyeth, John A., 45, 49

Meet the Author

LOCHLAINN SEABROOK, winner of the Jefferson Davis Historical Gold Medal for his "masterpiece," *A Rebel Born: A Defense of Nathan Bedford Forrest*, is an unreconstructed Southern historian, award-winning author, Civil War scholar, and traditional Southern Agrarian of Scottish, English, Irish, Welsh, German, and Italian extraction. An encyclopedist, lexicographer, anthologist, musician, artist, graphic designer, genealogist, and photographer, as well as an award-winning poet, songwriter, and screenwriter, he has a thirty year background in historical nonfiction writing and is a member of the Sons of Confederate Veterans, the Civil War Trust, and the National Grange.

Due to similarities in their writing styles, ideas, and literary works, Seabrook is referred to as the "American ROBERT GRAVES," after his cousin, the prolific English writer, historian, mythographer, poet, and author of the classic tomes *The White Goddess* and *The Greek Myths*.

The grandson of an Appalachian coal-mining family, Seabrook is a seventh-generation Kentuckian, co-chair of the Jent/Gent Family Committee (Kentucky), founder and director of the Blakeney Family Tree Project, and a board member of the Friends of Colonel Benjamin E. Caudill. Seabrook's literary works have been endorsed by leading authorities, museum curators, award-winning historians, bestselling authors, celebrities, noted scientists, TV show hosts, well respected educators, renown military artists, esteemed Southern organizations, and distinguished academicians from around the world.

(Image © Sea Raven Press)

He has authored some thirty popular adult and teen books specializing in the following topics: the American Civil War, pro-South studies, Confederate biographies, anthologies, and histories, genealogical monographs, theology, thealogy, Jesus and the Bible, self-help, healing, health, anthropology, ghost stories, the paranormal, family histories, military encyclopedias, etymological dictionaries, ufology, social issues, comparative analysis of the origins of Christmas, and cross-cultural studies of the family and marriage.

His eight children's books include a Southern children's guide to the Civil War, a dictionary of religion and myth, a rewriting of the King Arthur legend (which reinstates the original pre-Christian motifs), two bedtime stories for preschoolers, a naturalist's guidebook to owls, a worldwide look at the family, and an examination of the Near-Death Experience.

Of blue-blooded Southern stock through his Kentucky, Tennessee, Virginia, West Virginia, and North Carolina ancestors, he is a direct descendant of European royalty via his 6th great-grandfather, the EARL OF OXFORD, after which London's famous Harley Street is named. Among his celebrated male Celtic ancestors is ROBERT THE BRUCE, King of Scotland, Seabrook's 22nd great-grandfather. The 21st great-grandson of EDWARD I "LONGSHANKS" PLANTAGENET), King of England, Seabrook is a thirteenth-generation Southerner through his descent from the colonists of Jamestown, Virginia (1607).

Seabrook is related to numerous Confederate icons and other 19th-Century luminaries, among them: ROBERT E. LEE, NATHAN BEDFORD FORREST, STONEWALL JACKSON, ALEXANDER H. STEPHENS, JESSE JAMES, JEB STUART, JOHN HUNT MORGAN, NATHANIEL F. CHEAIRS, EDMUND W. RUCKER, STATES RIGHTS GIST, RICHARD TAYLOR, JOHN S. MOSBY, JOHN B. WOMACK, PIERRE G. T. BEAUREGARD, JOHN BELL HOOD, JAMES LONGSTREET, GEORGE W. GORDON, THEODRICK "TOD" CARTER, ABRAM POINDEXTER MAURY, WILLIAM GILES HARDING, JOHN W. MCGAVOCK, JOHN LAWTON SEABROOK, and MARY CHESNUT.

A cousin The 2nd, 3rd, and 4th great-grandson of dozens of Confederate soldiers, one of his closest connections to the War for Southern Independence is through his 3rd great-grandfather, ELIAS JENT, SR., who fought for the Confederacy in the Thirteenth Cavalry Kentucky under Seabrook's 2nd cousin, Colonel BENJAMIN E. CAUDILL. The Thirteenth, also known as "Caudill's Army," fought in numerous conflicts, including the Battles of Saltville, Gladsville, Mill Cliff, Poor Fork, Whitesburg, and Leatherwood.

(Image © Lochlainn Seabrook)

Born with music in his blood, Seabrook is an award-winning, multi-genre, BMI-Nashville songwriter and lyricist who has composed some 3,000 songs (250 albums), and whose original music has been heard on TV and radio worldwide. In 2012 his poignant ballad *That's My Girl*—recorded and produced by JOHN CARTER CASH (son of JOHNNY CASH and executive producer of the five-time Academy Award-winning film *Walk the Line*)—was selected for inclusion in the film *Cowgirls N' Angels*, starring BAILEE MADISON, JACKSON RATHBONE, and JAMES CROMWELL.

A musician, producer, multi-instrumentalist, and renown performer—whose keyboard work has been variously compared to pianists from HARGUS ROBBINS and VINCE GUARALDI to ELTON JOHN and LEONARD BERNSTEIN—Seabrook has opened for groups such as the EARL SCRUGGS REVIEW, TED NUGENT, and BOB SEGER, and has performed privately for such public figures as PRESIDENT RONALD REAGAN, BURT REYNOLDS, and SENATOR EDWARD W. BROOKE.

Seabrook's cousins in the entertainment business include: JOHNNY CASH, ELVIS PRESLEY, BILLY RAY and MILEY CYRUS, PATTY LOVELESS, TIM MCGRAW, LEE ANN WOMACK, DOLLY PARTON, REESE WITHERSPOON, PAT BOONE, NAOMI, WYNONNA, and ASHLEY JUDD, RICKY SKAGGS, THE SUNSHINE SISTERS, TOM CRUISE, MARTHA CARSON, and CHET ATKINS.

Seabrook lives with his wife and family in historic Middle Tennessee, the heart of the Confederacy, where his conservative Southern ancestors fought valiantly against liberal Lincoln and the progressive North in defense of Jeffersonianism, constitutional government, and personal liberty.

LOCHLAINNSEABROOK.COM

Meet the Cover Artist

For over 30 years American artist **JOHN PAUL STRAIN** has been amazing art collectors with his unique talent of capturing moments in time from the early days of the American Frontier, the glory and pageantry of the American Civil War, to contemporary scenic and romantic locations across the world. From the early age of twenty-one, Mr. Strain's paintings were represented by Trailside Galleries, America's most prestigious western art gallery. For fifteen years his beautiful landscapes, wild life paintings, and depictions of Indian life were represented by most every major western art gallery and top art auctions in the United States.

(Image © John Paul Strain)

In 1991 Mr. Strain broadened his subjects to include historical art of the American Civil War. During the next seventeen years he focused his work on the world of daring horseback raids and epic battles with great armies and leaders, capturing and preserving a unique era in history. Over a period of years, Mr. Strain became known as America's leading historical artist, with over fifty magazine covers featuring his paintings.

His work is featured in books, movies, and film. Mr. Strain's book, *A Witness to the Civil War*, released in November 2002, was a best seller for his publisher and quickly sold out of it's first printing. The book is unusual among art books in that it is written by the artist. The Scholastic Resources Company purchased over 3,000 copies of the edition for school libraries across the US. His new book is scheduled to be released in 2009.

Strain's paintings have helped to raise funds for many historical restoration projects and battlefield preservation organizations. The National Park Service uses his images in their publications and at battlefield sites. A number of historical private institutions have on site displays featuring his work such as General JEB Stuart's home and estate, and General Jubal Early's boyhood home.

Mr. Strain and his paintings were also featured on the television shows of C-Span's Washington Journal, The History Channel, and Extreme Makeover Home Edition. Throughout his career he has won many awards for his art.

Reproductions of his work have won numerous first place awards and "Best of Show" honors, such as the PICA Awards, The Printing Industry of the Carolinas, and just recently at the PIAG 2008 Awards in Georgia, he won the Top Gold Award for his painting "New Year's Wish," and Best Of Category Giclée for "Fire In the Sky."

Strain is also a featured artist for internationally know collector art companies the Bradford Exchange and the Franklin Mint, where he has created a Civil War Chess Set, several limited edition plate series, sculptures, and many other collectable items featuring his paintings. Mr. Strain has also completed a number of commissioned works for the United States Army, which are on permanent display at Fort Leavenworth, Kansas, Fort McNair, Washington, D.C., and the battlefield visitor's center at Normandy, France.

Today, Mr. Strain's original paintings can be found in many noted museums such as the Museum of Fredericksburg, South Georgia Relics Museum, and at Thomas Jefferson's home, Monticello. His work is included in many private fine art collections, corporate collections, and is owned by dignitaries such as United States Senators, Congressmen and a number of State Governors.

JohnPaulStrain.com

If you enjoyed this book you will want to own Mr. Seabrook's complete set:
"THE NATHAN BEDFORD FORREST BOOK COLLECTION"

A REBEL BORN: A DEFENSE OF NATHAN BEDFORD FORREST
GIVE 'EM HELL BOYS! THE COMPLETE MILITARY CORRESPONDENCE OF NATHAN BEDFORD FORREST
SADDLE, SWORD, AND GUN: A BIOGRAPHY OF NATHAN BEDFORD FORREST FOR TEENS
FORREST! 99 REASONS TO LOVE NATHAN BEDFORD FORREST
NATHAN BEDFORD FORREST: CONFEDERATE HERO, AMERICAN PATRIOT
THE QUOTABLE NATHAN BEDFORD FORREST

Available from Sea Raven Press and wherever fine books are sold.

All book covers are available as 11" X 17" prints, suitable for framing

SeaRavenPress.com

www.ingramcontent.com/pod-product-compliance
Lightning Source LLC
LaVergne TN
LVHW041230080426
835508LV00011B/1133